Book of
Canadian
Wine

Book of Canadian Wine

Melissa Priestley

BLUE
BIKE
BOOKS

The Publisher: Blue Bike Books
Website: www.bluebikebooks.com

Library and Archives Canada Cataloguing in Publication

Priestley, Melissa, 1984–
        Book of Canadian wine / by Melissa Priestley.

Includes bibliographical references.
ISBN 978-1-897278-62-8

        1. Wine and wine making—Canada—Miscellanea. 2. Wine and wine
making—Canada—History. I. Title.

TP559.C3P75 2009   641.2'20971   C2009-900183-7

Project Director: Nicholle Carrière
Project Editor: Pat Price
Cover Image: Photos.com
Illustrations: Roger Garcia
Photo Credits: Courtesy of: Chateau des Charmes (p. 92); Domaine de Chaberton
(p. 76, 80, 116, 152,); Domaine Pinnacle (p. 173); Elephant Island Orchard Wines
(p. 164); Ex Nihilo Winery: (p. 132, Stephanie Tracey [photography], Chip Sheean
Designs [design], "Rolling Stones" and Tongue and Lip Design are trademarks of
Musidor B.V.); Henry of Pelham Family Estate Winery (p. 62, 69, 143, 146);
John Howard Cellars of Distinction, Brandever Design (p. 122), Jost Vineyards
(p. 107); Pelee Island Winery (p. 21, 97, 187); photos.com (p. 48, 86, 138, 194);
Melissa Priestley (p. 130, 166); Summerhill Pyramid Winery (p. 180, 208);
Vincor Canada (p. 8, 12, 39, 42, 52, 66, 72, 110, 184).

We acknowledge the support of the Alberta Foundation for the Arts for our
publishing program.
We acknowledge the financial support of the Government of Canada through the Book
Publishing Industry Development Program (BPIDP) for our publishing activities.

Alberta Foundation for the Arts

Canadian Heritage   Patrimoine canadien

ACKNOWLEDGEMENTS

I would like to extend my heartfelt thanks to the following
people:
Matt, for keeping me going.
Hayley, for our "study sessions."
Nick, for passing on the word.
Pat, for putting it back together.
To everyone else who had a hand in the project: thank you
very much—I raise a glass to all of you! (And I promise
I won't bombard you with Canadian wine trivia anymore.)

CONTENTS

FRUITFUL PURSUITS

WINE BY DESIGN

WINE 101

INTRODUCTION

In Canada, wine isn't made by reclusive old men in crumbling stone castles. Here, in a nation boasting the world's highest number of home winemakers, everyone seems to have a hand in the world of winemaking—even hockey players! Indeed, everyone from doctors and lawyers to famous actors have dipped their fingers into Canada's fermentation tank.

That's not to say there are no professional winemakers in Canada. On the contrary, Canada has its fair share of wine celebrities—and not the kind from Hollywood. Renowned winemakers from such illustrious wine regions as Burgundy in France and the Rhine Valley in Germany have pulled up their European roots and transplanted them in Canadian soil. Ontario's prestigious Brock University's viticulture program graduates hundreds of well-trained candidates every year. And located throughout the wine-growing regions are several technical research institutes that continually make advancements in Canadian grape-growing and winemaking technology.

But there's much more to Canada's wine industry than famous faces and university programs. Wineries are sites of Canadian history. All manner of weird and wonderful events have happened in and around the areas in which grapes grow—and they still do. History is in the making at many Canadian wineries, from the construction of Frank Gehry–designed winery buildings to the high-flying adventures of winemaking amateur pilots.

I urge you to check out Canada's wine offerings, even if you have no prior experience with wine. After all, wine is simply fermented grape juice! There's room for everyone in the Canadian wine world.

CANADA'S FIRST WINEMAKERS

Vinland, Vinland

Grapevines have been around since Canada's early days. In fact, before the country was called Canada, it had another name: Vinland, or Land of Wine. In about 1000 AD, Norse explorers arrived in what is now L'Anse aux Meadows, on the coast of Newfoundland. Their leader, Leif Eriksson, established a settlement and christened the area with a name that described the many wild grapevines he found growing there.

DID YOU  KNOW?

L'Anse aux Meadows is the earliest-known European settlement in the New World. The archaeological remains of three Norse buildings can still be seen, and the entire site was declared a UNESCO World Heritage Site in 1978.

Viking Vintners
The details of Eriksson's journey across the Atlantic and settlement at L'Anse aux Meadows are outlined in the *Saga of the Greenlanders,* an Icelandic saga that dates to the 13th century. Eriksson and his crew stayed in Vinland for the winter and departed the next summer, heading back to Greenland with a plentiful supply of lumber and grapes. Although we don't know for sure, these grapes were probably in raisin or wine form, the only way they could have survived the long sea voyage. After all, the Vikings did name the country Land of Wine, not Land of Grapes!

Land of Blueberries?

If you've ever been to Newfoundland, you'll know that grapevines are not a common sight. When the province isn't covered in snow, you're more likely to see fields of blueberries than rows of grapevines. Some people argue that Eriksson's grapes were actually blueberries, which grow rampant throughout the Maritimes. However, the world was a warmer place in Eriksson's era—the Earth went through a period of unusually warm temperatures from 1000 to 1300 AD. In fact, in those days, the Vikings were able to farm parts of Greenland that are now virtually inhospitable. Eriksson landed on Canada's shores near the beginning of this warm spell. Because these warm temperatures would have allowed grapevines to grow easily, it's possible that Eriksson actually did find grapes, not blueberries.

Winery Profile Nk'Mip Cellars

Canada's aboriginals are very much involved in today's winemaking industry. Nk'Mip (pronounced in-ka-meep) Cellars in the Okanagan has led the way. The winery, located in the south Okanagan Valley on Lake Osoyoos, is owned by the Osoyoos Indian Band. Although the winery has only been operating since 2002, the band has been running Inkameep Vineyards since 1968. These vineyards are some of the Okanagan Valley's first plantings of *Vitis vinifera* grapes (the species responsible for all the world's top-quality wines; *Vitis* is Latin for "grapevine," and *vinifera* refers to the specific species of grape).

For the last 40 years, Inkameep Vineyards has supplied all the main Okanagan producers with grapes. Starting a winery to capitalize on their supply of premium grapes was a natural step for the band, which hasn't looked back since. The winery's very first wines won gold medals in national competitions, and there isn't a single wine in the winery's portfolio that has not won an award—not bad for a winery that's less than a decade old.

DID YOU  KNOW?

The Nk'Mip winery was initially supposed to be a casino, but when that proposal was rejected by the government, plans were quickly redrafted for a winery.

Wine for Wisachgimi

Although we have no archaeological evidence that wine was made by Canada's aboriginal peoples, there is a record of a ceremony called Wisachgimi, which means "place of grapes." In the centuries before colonization, the Seneca, Tuscarora and Cayuga tribes brought an annual gift of grape juice to the water gods that dwelt below Niagara Falls. No one knows if this juice was fermented or not, but many have suggested that, even if it started out in a pre-fermented state, it would have become wine eventually. The journey from the tribes' settlements to Niagara Falls would have been long and hot, and the grape juice would have fermented along the way, turning into a crude form of wine. This means the ceremony's participants were Canada's first (accidental) winemakers—unless Eriksson and his crew beat them to it, of course.

Cartier's Calling

The Vikings and aboriginals weren't the only ones to come up with names describing Canada as a land of grapes. When Jacques Cartier arrived in Canada in 1535, south of the Vikings' landing spot, in Québec, he came up with a similarly grapey name for the area: Île de Bacchus, or Island of Bacchus, for the Roman god of wine. Now, it might be somewhat plausible for the Norse to confuse a blueberry with a grape—even someone as well-travelled as Eriksson—but you certainly can't argue that the French would make the same mistake.

As a side note, in a sudden fit of patriotism—or perhaps self-preservation—Cartier changed the name of the island to Île d'Orleans, in honour of the son of his royal patron, the Duc d'Orleans. But that first name shows where his passions truly were....

DID YOU  KNOW?

There are three wineries on Île d'Orleans: Vignoble de Sainte-Petronille, Vignoble Isle de Bacchus and Vignoble Domaine de la Source à Marguerite.

Grape Mistake

Marc Lescarbot, a French lawyer and historian who spent a year at Port Royal, Nova Scotia, in 1606–07, hoped to be Nova Scotia's first vigneron but was cheated out of his dream by an absent-minded shipmate. Lescarbot had discovered grapevines along the coast in New Brunswick and had taken a sample of them with the intention of planting them at Port Royal. However, the bundle of vines was forgotten by a valet.

Canada's First Vines

The first vineyard in Canada was planted by French settlers in Nova Scotia in 1633, when high-ranking naval officer Isaac de Razilly set up the outpost of Fort-Ste-Marie-de-Grace (now LaHave). The following year, de Razilly wrote to Lescarbot, who had by then returned to France: "I have planted some vines as they do in Bordeaux which come along very well…Vines grow here naturally. The wine made from these has been used to celebrate mass." The vines were used to make sacramental wine until the expulsion of the Acadians in 1755, which brought an end to winemaking in the area.

Jesuit Winemakers

The first official written record of winemaking in Canada is in Paul Le Jeune's *Relation of the Jesuits*, a manuscript from 1636. The *Relations* were annual reports compiled by the Jesuit priests in the missions in New France and sent back to Paris. Le Jeune notes that "in some places there are many wild vines loaded with grapes; some have made wine of them through curiosity. I tasted it, and it seems to be very good. Many are sure that the vine would succeed here; and, when I urged against this the rigor of the cold, they replied that the vine-stock will be safe all winter under the snow, and that in the spring it need not be feared that the vines will freeze as they do in France, because they will not sprout so early."

Le Jeune was not the only one to encourage winemaking. In 1668, Father Jacques Bruyas, a Jesuit missionary working with Iroquois missions in Québec, wrote: "If one were to take some trouble to plant some vines and trees, they would yield as well as they do in France...and (properly pruned) the grapes would be as good as those of France."

Canada's First Watering Hole

Canada's first inn was established in Québec City in 1648, when the Council of New France granted Jacques Boisdon the right to open an inn and serve alcoholic beverages. However, Boisdon was subject to numerous regulations, chief among them the stipulation that the inn be located within sight of the church. Apparently, having the inn reside within the sight of God was thought to be a deterrent against drunkenness, scandal and blasphemy. The inn was also subject to stringent laws relating to its hours of operation—obviously, it had to be closed on Sunday. Despite these regulations, the Council helped Boisdon establish his venture by providing him with an initial supply of eight barrels of French wine, free of charge. Even they must have been getting a little thirsty.

DID YOU KNOW?

Whiskey, not wine, was the drink of choice of early Canadians, even government officials—Canada's first prime minister, Sir John A. Macdonald, reputedly indulged in "gargantuan" whiskey-drinking bouts.

Sour Grapes?

Wine made from native grapes didn't go over well with Canada's early settlers. Although the wine was tolerable for mass, it didn't pass muster as table wine. The upper classes drank red wine imported from Europe; the rest of the populace had to make do with crude spirits and beer, made from whatever produce was available at the time.

Spreading the Vine

The Church played a part in every New World wine industry, including Canada's. Although the early missionary priests brought a supply of wine with them from Europe, they began making wine in their New World colonies to ensure that they had a plentiful supply on hand. Shipping wine from Europe was costly and took a long time; often, the wine didn't fare well over the long sea voyage and was little more than vinegar by the time it reached the New World. So, in the 1600s, the missionaries, primarily the Jesuits, began bringing cuttings from Europe to the missions in Ontario, Québec and British Columbia. However, though records show that wine was made by the mission priests, none was ever sold commercially; wine was used solely for religious ceremonies and the priests' personal use.

The Jesuits were also responsible for the first winemaking efforts throughout Spain's South American colonies, in particular Peru, Chile and Argentina, in the 1500s. In California, a Franciscan missionary named Junípero Serra established the first vineyard and winery there in 1769.

DID YOU KNOW?

A common drink of the early settlers was spruce beer, made from fir branches.

Father of the Canadian Wine Industry

Canada's wine industry didn't really get going until the 1800s. Most credit Johann Schiller, a former corporal, with being the father of Canada's wine industry. For his service to the British military in Canada, the Crown granted Schiller eight hectares of land in Cooksville, Ontario (now part of Mississauga). Schiller had gained valuable winemaking experience growing vines in his homeland, Germany's Rhine Valley—one of Europe's renowned wine regions.

After settling in Ontario and discovering wild grapevines growing along the banks of the nearby Credit River, Schiller transplanted several to a small vineyard behind his house. By 1811, he had domesticated the wild grapevines and supplemented his vineyard with native vines purchased from the United States. Although he didn't practice his operation on a commercial scale, he did make enough wine to sell some to his neighbours. He must have been quite popular!

As a winemaker, Schiller was way ahead of his time. The next record of winemaking doesn't occur until four decades after Schiller's precocious efforts. Although others must have been experimenting with grapevines, it wasn't until the 1850s that articles on winemaking began cropping up in governmental papers and agricultural publications.

The Optimist Count

Settlers in Québec experimented with planting European grape varieties throughout the 18th and 19th centuries, led by such adamant supporters as Count Justin de Courtenay, a French nobleman, who was convinced that Canada could produce wines rivalling those of France. De Courtenay's industrious example set the standard for Québec vintners, who needed to be a resilient lot to successfully endure the many setbacks of farming in the province's harsh climate.

De Courtenay moved to Ontario in 1864, where he resurrected Johann Schiller's vineyard, doubling its size and naming it the Vine Growers Association. He sold wines under the label Clair House, and they even travelled as far as Paris—Clair House wines appeared in a Paris exhibition celebrating Canada's nationhood in 1867.

DID YOU  KNOW?

By the early 1860s, Québec already had more than 30 vineyards growing grapes on more than 40 hectares of land. By 1935, the province had only two hectares of vines left.

Wine Decline

Québec's wine industry began to wane towards the end of the 19th century. Despite the best efforts of the early pioneers, their vines were ill-fated. By the turn of the century, the vast majority of all vines had been killed off by the winter cold. Prohibition provided the final nail in the coffin; the growing temperance movement succeeded in quashing much of the industry.

Mission Vines

In British Columbia, the first to plant wine grapes was Father Charles Pandosy, an Oblate missionary who founded the first European settlement in the Okanagan Valley. In 1860, he obtained vines from an Oblate mission in Oregon and planted them at his mission, in the area that is now East Kelowna. Pandosy was not the founder of the BC wine industry, however. There is no record of the mission fathers making wine from these vines, and, even if they did, none was ever released commercially; it would have been used for sacramental purposes only. There's no evidence that the mission propagated any other vineyards, either.

Grapes for Eating, Not for Drinking

Nova Scotia produced table grapes long before it began experimenting with wine grapes. In the early 1800s, an English settler, Charles Prescott, imported and grew grapes on his farm in the Annapolis Valley (one of Nova Scotia's main grape-growing areas). However, there is no mention of whether Prescott ever made wine from these grapes.

The table-grape industry thrived in Nova Scotia throughout the 19th century. Many family farms in the Annapolis Valley and along the South Shore grew table grapes. Although many of these farmers must have undoubtedly made wine from their leftover crops, the province's first commercial winery didn't open until more than a century later.

Grape Jelly

Although Ontario boasted 35 commercial wineries by 1890, most were very small operations. Grape growing was often a side project for farmers wanting to diversify. Most of these grapes were destined to be eaten, not made into wine, and the grape varieties commonly grown for eating didn't make very good wine. Concord grapes were a perennial favourite; they're delicious when fresh or made into jam or jelly, but Concord grape wine is only tolerable to those truly desperate for a drink—or who have no taste buds.

Island Wine

Canada's first commercial winery was Vin Villa on Ontario's Pelee Island, located in the Western Basin of Lake Erie, which opened its cellar doors in 1866. The winery was the brainchild of a group of Americans from Kentucky, who had been in the grape business for more than a decade. D.J. Williams, Thomas Williams and Thaddeus Smith purchased a farm on the island and planted 12 hectares of vines. Before they even built a house, they excavated a large wine cellar—clearly, they weren't there to fool around. The men formed a partnership with an enterprising grocer on the mainland, Major J.S. Hamilton. Hamilton, who, in 1871, was granted a royal charter to sell wine and liquor, purchased grapes and wine from Vin Villa. In fact, Hamilton had such high aspirations that he eventually took over Vin Villa.

Although the winery no longer exists, Vin Villa's original stone ruins can still be seen. Wine has remained an important part of

Pelee Island's heritage since those early days; the island is home to the biggest estate winery in Canada, with more than 243 hectares of grapevines.

DID YOU  KNOW?

Pelee Island is Canada's southernmost point. It is on the same latitude as northern California and is closer to the equator than Rome, Italy.

Enduring Enterprises

Despite the dubious quality of their wines, a few of Ontario's early wineries remained in operation for more than a century. One of these was George Barnes' winery, which opened in 1873 in St. Catharines. The winery's original name was the Ontario Grape Growing and Wine Manufacturing Company, Limited. Although long-winded and not terribly poetic, the name certainly provided a clear picture of the company's purpose. The name was changed to Barnes Wines a few years later. The winery continued to produce wine until 1988, when it was purchased by Château-Gai.

T.G. Bright and Company was another long-lived winery pioneer. Initially called Niagara Falls Wine Company, the winery opened in 1874 and lasted well into the late 20th century. In 1993, Brights merged with Inniskillin Wines to form Vincor International, Canada's largest wine company.

PROHIBITION

Man versus Alcohol

Prohibition in Canada was the ultimate result of temperance movements that began in the late 1800s. Temperance movements placed the consumption of alcohol at the root of almost all social problems—especially the poverty, unemployment and crime that began increasing dramatically in the 19th century, as the population became urbanized. The movement gained further momentum with the acknowledgment from the medical community that drinking too much alcohol had negative effects on physical and psychological health.

Temperate Times

Canada's Temperance Movement (the popular support movement behind Prohibition) began about the same time as its counterpart in the United States, at the end of the 19th century and the beginning of the 20th century—peaking with the introduction of Prohibition (the actual period in which alcohol was banned) around the 1920s. However, unlike the United States, which banned the sale, manufacture and transportation of alcohol on a national level, Canada's Prohibition laws differed from province to province. This country also experienced a shorter dry period than did the United States, where Prohibition lasted from 1919 to 1933. Most provinces began Prohibition in the 1920s and repealed it within a decade.

DID YOU KNOW?

A national referendum on the issue of Prohibition was held in 1898. All provinces voted for Prohibition, except Québec— more than 81 percent of Québecers voted against it.

A Growing Concern

In 1916, the Ontario government passed the Ontario Temperance Act, which remained in effect until 1927. The Act stipulated that alcohol could only be sold with permission from the province. This allowed industrial alcohol to be produced for the war effort—among other things, it was used to make explosives, bringing a whole new meaning to the term "firewater." Producers and purveyors of commercial beverage alcohol were not granted permission, however, making the sale of alcoholic beverages illegal. All drinking establishments were closed, and stores could not sell any alcoholic products. But because grape growing was a huge industry in Ontario, growers had a lot of political clout, and they managed to pressure the government to exempt wineries from the Temperance Act. With a government permit, wineries could make wine and sell it in a store attached to the winemaking premises. In one fell swoop, wine became the entire province's drink of choice.

DID YOU  KNOW?

During Prohibition in Ontario, there was a limit on the minimum purchase of wine: individuals had to buy at least a five-gallon keg or a case of 12 bottles—not exactly a small amount by most standards, especially during such a "temperate" time.

Prohibition Pandemonium

Because Canadian liquor laws are enforced by the provincial governments, Prohibition was implemented at different times in the various provinces:

British Columbia: 1917–21

Alberta 1916–23

Saskatchewan: 1917–24

Manitoba: 1916–23

Ontario: 1916–27

Québec: 1919

Newfoundland: 1917–25

New Brunswick: 1917–27

Nova Scotia: 1915–29

Prince Edward Island: 1901–48

For the most part, Prohibition did not last long in any of the provinces. However, with the exception of Ontario, none of the provinces were allowed exceptions to the Temperance Acts, and the sale of all alcoholic beverages, including wine, was illegal.

Prohibition Escapee

Québec was a notable exception to Canada's period of Prohibition. The Parliament of Québec enacted Prohibition on May 1, 1919—but it only lasted a few weeks. Intense public pressure resulted in a provincial referendum, and the majority of Québecers voted to exclude beer, wine and cider from the list of banned substances. This effectively made Québec the only region in North America to escape an extended period of prohibition. In general, consuming alcohol was (and still is) far more socially acceptable in Europe than in Canada; Québec's predominantly French population is part of a centuries-old culture in which drinking is seen in a much different light.

PEI: Dry as a Desert

At the opposite end of the spectrum from Québec was Prince
Edward Island. PEI was the first province in Canada to pass
Prohibition; it started just after the turn of the century in 1901.
This dry spell was the longest in Canadian history, lasting
almost half a century; repeal in PEI did not occur until 1948.

Cure for the Common Cold

Because making wine for medicinal purposes was allowed
during Prohibition, prescriptions for "medicine" containing
a hefty dose of alcohol suddenly became easy to get. Canadian
writer and humorist Stephen Leacock is noted for making

a comment on the rampant
use of alcohol for so-called
medicinal purposes: "To get
a drink during Prohibition
it is necessary to go to the
drug store…and lean up
against the counter mak-
ing a gurgling sigh
like apoplexy. One
often sees there
apoplexy cases
lined up
four deep."

To combat the wanton use of booze as medicine, the Canadian government passed legislation requiring producers of these "medications" to add an emetic—a substance that induces vomiting. Consuming more than the recommended dose caused the "patient" to quickly lose his lunch and, needless to say, the desire to drink. This strategy worked perfectly, and the consumption of medicinal wine quickly tapered off.

Running Rampant

The exemption of wine in the Ontario Temperance Act resulted in an explosion of new wineries. During Prohibition in Ontario, the number of wineries in the province increased to 67 from 10. Licences were handed out like candy to anyone who asked, and the volume of wine produced increased exponentially. However, the quality of the wine was poor; more than 80 percent was port-style wine that was high in alcohol and made from Concord grapes.

DID YOU  KNOW?

In 1920, Canadians consumed 840,304 litres (221,985 gallons) of domestic wine. By 1930, that figure had risen to 8,361,244 litres (2,208,807 gallons)—for Ontario alone.

Rivers of Plonk

Throughout Prohibition, the majority of Ontario's wineries engaged in many unscrupulous practices. At the time, the provincial government did not enforce inspections and had no food and drug act; nobody asked questions, so there was no quality control. By the time Ontario's Prohibition was repealed in 1927, the uncontrolled growth of the wine industry had resulted in dozens of new wineries, which flooded the province with rivers of barely drinkable—and, in some cases, even dangerous—wine. Most, if not all, of the wine was extremely diluted. Growers stretched their crops to ridiculous amounts; 2271 litres (600 gallons) of wine were produced from only one ton of grapes—more than double the current legal limit. Because so much water was added, dyes had to be used to colour the wine. Some of these additives were innocuous, vegetable-based colourings, but a distressing amount of coal-tar dye was also used.

DID YOU KNOW?

During Prohibition, producers added such dodgy substances as coal-tar dye, salicylic acid, saccharin and even formaldehyde to their wines, in an attempt to mask disagreeable colours, aromas and flavours.

Stemming the Bad Wine Tide
To clean up the industry, the Ontario government introduced the Liquor Control Act in 1927 to regulate the sale of alcohol. The Act also instituted a series of laws to improve the quality of wine. One ruling limited the amount of volatile acid—a compound that makes the wine smell and taste like vinegar—permitted in wine, which immediately got rid of half of the Prohibition-style plonk. Over the next few years, other laws were introduced; the result was better wine—and more and more winery closures.

Economic Shambles

The economic impact of Prohibition was extremely damaging in Ontario, especially on the wine trade. Although wine producers enjoyed record profits during the free-for-all, the end of Prohibition shifted consumer buying patterns away from winery retail stores—alcohol was now available at stores in cities and towns, and with the increasing urbanization of Ontario's population, the wineries lost a huge portion of their revenue. Because Repeal occurred during the Depression, sales were already low.

Strange Liquor Laws

Even after Prohibition was repealed in Ontario, many strange and seemingly arbitrary laws were enacted to curb overconsumption. Many of these laws were kept in place for decades, until well into the 1970s. Here is a list of some of the more unusual ones:

- ☞ Bars were required to have a separate room for women, who could only enter and have a drink if accompanied by a male.

- ☞ Bar patrons were forbidden to hold a drink while standing. A customer wanting to change tables had to have a waiter move his glass for him.

- ☞ Under the Lord's Day Act, all bars and liquor stores had to remain closed all Sunday, starting at midnight on Saturday. Restaurants could only serve alcohol if it was accompanied by food.

- ☞ Restaurants were forbidden to use alcohol for cooking.

- ☞ All alcoholic products had to be transported in a plain brown paper bag.

Other provinces emerged from Prohibition with similarly strict laws. In Saskatchewan, liquor could be served in a restaurant only if at least six main courses were offered; to be served a drink, restaurant patrons were required to be seated; and drinks could only be ordered with a meal. It was also illegal to drink alcohol while watching exotic dancers.

Until the 1980s, British Columbia and Alberta were governed by Acts similar to Ontario's Lord's Day Act, which required that liquor stores remain closed on Sundays. Also, alcohol could only be served with a meal. Alberta privatized the sale of liquor in 1994, taking a definitive step away from the governmental control implemented just after Prohibition. However, although private wine and beer stores exist in BC and Ontario, those provinces continue to be dominated by the large government-run stores.

Censorship of the (Wine) Press

Although it seems rather ridiculous now, during the 1950s and '60s, the *St. Catharines Standard* (a daily newspaper in St. Catharines, Ontario) deliberately removed the word "wine" from all references to the Niagara Grape and Wine Festival, which began in the early 1950s. This censorship was part of the hangover from Prohibition. Thankfully, omitting the word "wine" had little detrimental effect on the festival, which celebrated its 58th anniversary in 2009. The *St. Catharines Standard* is also still around, though it no longer censors wine references in its festival coverage.

BOOTLEG BOOZE

Alberta Alcohol

Prohibiting alcohol in written law is one thing; enforcing it in the real world is another. Bootlegging and rum-running (the term used to describe bootlegging over water) increased exponentially during Prohibition. Although bootlegging and rum-running occurred throughout North America, there were a few epicentres of activity, one of which was Whiskey Gap, Alberta—really, the name says it all. This small town was the site of a large bootlegging operation, in which huge quantities of alcohol were smuggled across the border from the United States into Canada, starting in 1916, when Alberta enacted Prohibition. Things changed in the latter half of the 1920s: Alberta repealed Prohibition in 1924, and the United States remained dry until 1933—so Albertans returned the favour by shipping alcohol south.

DID YOU  KNOW?

The term "bootleg" is thought to have originated from the practice of concealing flasks of alcohol in high-top boots, commonly worn by women in the 1920s.

Little Chicago

Although you might not expect the town of Moose Jaw, Saskatchewan, to be a hot spot of organized crime, during Prohibition, the town became known as "Little Chicago," thanks to an influx of American mobsters engaged in bootlegging. Because the Soo railroad line ran from Chicago to Moose Jaw, it was easy for bootleggers to smuggle Canadian liquor south across the border. The town became a miniature

Las Vegas during the 1920s, with gambling and prostitution running rampant throughout the town's 23 hotels and night-clubs. An extensive network of underground tunnels was built below Moose Jaw in the 1880s by Chinese railroad workers, many of whom were illegal immigrants. During Prohibition, these tunnels were used to hide bootleg liquor. Today, they're a tourist attraction, where visitors are taken on tours by actors in period costumes.

DID YOU  KNOW?

Rumour has it that, during Prohibition, Chicago mob king Al Capone visited Moose Jaw to oversee his bootlegging operations.

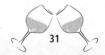

Gangster Ingenuity

Prohibition-era bootleggers found creative ways of transporting illegal booze across the border and hiding it from the Prohibition agents and customs officials. Cars with false floors and false gas tanks were often used; sometimes even the tires were filled with whiskey, instead of air! Smugglers commonly employed locals, especially families with small children who were less likely to raise suspicion, to drive the cars over the border. Car swaps were another frequent tactic: two identical cars were driven to the border, where their licence plates were switched, should the bootlegger's car have aroused suspicion. While the decoy car was intercepted by the border patrol and searched, the car containing the alcohol quickly disappeared down the highway. Desperate bootleggers even resorted to carrying liquor across the border on foot and horseback.

DID YOU KNOW?

Prince Edward Island was a favourite destination for rum-runners during the province's decades-long alcohol ban.

Purple Power Play

The Great Lakes were a hotbed of rum-running during Prohibition—the maze of islands and channels provided perfect places for smugglers to hide their boats. Between 1927, when Prohibition was repealed in Ontario, and 1933, when it was repealed in the United States, a black-market pipeline of booze was established between cities on the Great Lakes. The border cities of Windsor, Sarnia and Detroit were epicentres of activity; bootleggers loaded up their boats in Windsor and Sarnia and then smuggled the booze across the waterways of Lake Erie, Lake St. Clair and the St. Clair River to Detroit.

The majority of these rum-running operations were led by the infamous Purple Gang, a Detroit-based crime organization led by Joe, Abe, Raymond and Izzy Bernstein. The gang had a reputation for being particularly ruthless and ambitious, hijacking other bootleggers they encountered on the lakes, by gunning them down and taking their cargo. During the 1920s, the estimated value of the Purple Gang's bootleg business from Canada to Detroit was worth more than $250 million per year.

DID YOU KNOW?

A line of ships located offshore, just outside the area patrolled by the Coast Guard—in the 1920s, in the Atlantic provinces, this was set at 19 kilometres—was called a rum row. Smaller, faster vessels met up with these "mother" ships, loaded up with a cargo of booze and then piloted back to shore.

Island Rum

During the 1920s, many of the coastal communities in New-foundland and Nova Scotia participated in trafficking booze across the border. The French islands of Miquelon and St. Pierre, in particular, were rum-running hubs. Located 26 kilometres off the coast of Newfoundland, they were far enough away from the mainland that authorities were rarely around. The islanders sold Canadian liquor to American bootleggers, who loaded up their ships on the islands and sailed south to American waters.

Coastal Crossings

In British Columbia, the proximity of Vancouver and Victoria to Seattle provided ample opportunity for rum-runners. Throughout the 1920s and early 1930s, an estimated 60 Canadian rum-runners smuggled liquor though BC's port cities to the United States.

DID YOU  KNOW?

Black-market booze still exists in Canada today—according to the Liquor Control Board of Ontario, as much as 11 percent of the sales of beverage alcohol in Ontario might be on the black market. That's a loss of more than $644 million in annual revenue.

THE GOOD: ICEWINE

Frozen Gold

Canada didn't invent icewine—that credit goes to Germany, which first began making icewine in the late 1700s. The creation was dubbed *eiswein*—literally "ice" and "wine" in German. However, Germany cannot make icewine regularly, because its winters aren't always cold enough. Canada, however, is the only wine-producing nation in the world with winters consistently cold enough to make icewine every year. (Many Canadians would probably say that these winters are too consistently cold.) More than any other wine, icewine is seen as uniquely Canadian. Trust Canadians to profit from ice.

Winter Winemaking

Icewine is made in the same way as regular wine, with a few noticeable differences. First, the grapes are picked and pressed when frozen. In Canada, icewine grapes must be harvested at a minimum temperature of –8°C, though many producers harvest at several degrees lower—the colder temperature results in a richer, more-concentrated juice. This is the coldest standard in the world; the minimum temperature for German icewine is –7°C.

This minimum temperature law means that the grapes are not harvested until well into December or January; harvests in February have even occurred in particularly warm years. The grapes are often picked at night and are usually pressed right in the field, so that they don't thaw; thawing dilutes the concentrated juice.

Second, because the sugar content of the grapes is so high, the fermentation process is much longer than regular wine, commonly taking several months to complete. It stops naturally when the wine is at about 10 to 12 percent alcohol per volume.

Happy Accident

When life gives you frozen grapes…make icewine? That's what Walter Hainle did. Hainle, a German textile salesman who took up winemaking as a hobby after emigrating to British Columbia, made Canada's first icewine in 1973, when an early winter froze the Okanagan vineyard from which he bought grapes. Calling on the icewine tradition from his homeland, Hainle saw the frozen grapes as an opportunity, rather than a misfortune. He very much enjoyed the results of this happy accident and began making icewine regularly.

Hainle turned his hobby into a serious profession when he planted a vineyard in the North Okanagan and sent his son to a wine school in Germany. In 1988, father and son opened Hainle Vineyards—and the first commercial Canadian icewine, from the 1978 vintage, was available for sale (Hainle had been cellaring many bottles of his previous vintages before opening the winery). Hainle still produces icewine, though no more than a few hundred litres per year.

DID YOU KNOW?

Roughly 75 percent of Canadian icewine hails from vineyards in Niagara.

Ontario's Specialty

Although the first icewine was made in the Okanagan, the majority of Canadian icewine comes from Ontario. The reason for this is purely a matter of nature. Although the temperature in both regions regularly drops below the minimum harvest temperature for icewine, the Okanagan often experiences one hard freeze, in which the temperature drops very low, very quickly. This is not ideal for icewine grapes, because they cannot be harvested when the temperature is too low—if the temperature is colder than –15°C, the grapes are hard as marbles and can even break the press.

In contrast, Niagara usually experiences a gentler freeze-and-thaw cycle, in which the temperatures will drop for a few days and then rise again. Although this can cause grief for the winemaker trying to decide when to call the icewine harvest, the finished product is usually better. The cycle of freezing and thawing, which dehydrates the grapes and concentrates their sugars, acids and extracts, intensifies the flavours and adds complexity to the wine.

DID YOU KNOW?

Inniskillin takes its name from the Royal Inniskilling Fusiliers, an Irish regiment that fought in the War of 1812. The winery is located on property granted to regiment member Colonel Cooper, for his service.

Award-winning Wine

Under Austrian winemaker Karl Kaiser's direction, Inniskillin Wines, another icewine pioneer, began making icewine in the early 1980s. Kaiser was trained in traditional winemaking techniques, including icewine production, through a private monastery school in Austria. Although a few other producers in Niagara were also experimenting with icewine, for several years only Inniskillin was able to make it in sufficient quantities to release it commercially.

A mere four years after releasing its first icewine, Inniskillin earned one of the most prestigious wine awards in the world: the Grand Prix d'Honneur was awarded to Inniskillin's 1989 Vidal Icewine at Vinexpo in Bordeaux, France. The award marked a huge milestone in Canadian wine history.

DID YOU KNOW?

Perhaps it's the multiple *i*'s or all the double letters in the name, but Inniskillin has been consistently misspelled throughout the winery's history. "Inniskillen" is the most common mistake; this spelling even appeared in the 51st annual report of the Liquor Control Board of Ontario.

Winery Profile **Inniskillin Wines**

Inniskillin was founded in 1975 by Donald Ziraldo and Karl Kaiser, who met rather serendipitously in the early 1970s. After obtaining a degree in agriculture from the University of Guelph, Ziraldo began working at his family's nursery, which specialized in fruit trees and grapevines. Kaiser, a native of Austria and long-time home winemaker, stopped at the nursery one day to buy some French hybrid grapevines. The two hit it off and soon found themselves planning their own winery.

☞

Winery Profile

The original Inniskillin winery was housed in an old shed at the Ziraldo nursery, until it moved to a more contemporary building in 1978—just down the road from the original. Although the winery has become synonymous with icewine, it has also established a reputation for Chardonnay, Pinot Noir and Riesling table wines. From its idealistic beginnings, the winery has become one of the cornerstones of the Canadian wine industry, with wineries in both Niagara and the Okanagan Valley. Inniskillin was acquired by Vincor International in 1995.

King of Frozen Grapes

The Vidal variety is the undisputed king of Canadian icewine grapes and is used in as much as 75 percent of the icewine made in Ontario. One of the reasons this grape makes such a good icewine is its thick skin. Like its *labrusca* relatives, Vidal's thick skin allows it to survive the freezing and thawing cycles without splitting, keeping the grape in perfect shape throughout the winter months. Vidal also has a high level of acidity, which balances the wine's intense sweetness.

DID YOU KNOW?

Vidal is the progeny of Ugni Blanc, a *vinifera* variety, and Rayon d'Or, a hybrid variety whose original name was Seibel 4986.

Frosty Favourites

Riesling is another icewine favourite. This comes as no surprise, given this variety's predominance in Germany, the world's other main producer of icewine. Riesling grapes are also quite high in acidity, which contributes to a balanced finished product.

Canada has also experimented, albeit on a very small scale, with such varieties as Chardonnay, Gewurztraminer, Ehrenfelser and Chenin Blanc. Some producers are even experimenting with Cabernet Franc, which makes an unusual red icewine.

The Flying Menace
The biggest threat to an icewine crop (and most regular wine crops, for that matter) is damage from birds. Although most vineyards employ some form of bird-control tactics throughout the growing season, such as propane cannons and other scaring devices, these are often not as effective once winter sets

in and the birds grow hungrier. Years with little snowfall are not as bad, because the birds have access to other sources of food. However, if there is enough snowfall to carpet everything in a solid layer of white, a vineyard full of exposed, overripe grapes is a hungry bird's paradise.

Starlings are the biggest offenders. In 1983, in an icewine pilot project, several Ontario producers set out to produce batches of icewine; two of them—Inniskillin and Reif—lost their entire crop to these birds. Hillebrand and Pelee Island were only a little more successful; the birds spared a few bunches, and the producers were able to harvest a small amount of grapes.

Net Profits

Although Canada's first attempts to make icewine were almost total losses, producers learned a valuable lesson in icewine production: protect the crop from birds or lose the whole thing. After their initial failure, Inniskillin took more extreme measures to protect its crop. This involved draping the vines with netting to keep the birds out, and it proved quite successful; Inniskillin's award-winning 1984 Vidal Icewine, its first icewine, marked a turning point in both the winery's and Canada's wine history.

A drive through Niagara's wine country in the winter months reveals long rows of bare vines incongruously loaded with ruddy bunches of grapes swathed in miles of wispy netting. However, not just any netting can be used. Starlings are innovative creatures, and hunger makes them even more desperate to get at a field of ripe fruit. The nets must be long enough to prevent the birds from getting at the fruit from underneath and from above.

Mesh size is also important. If it is too big, the birds can reach right through, but because machines are increasingly used to harvest the grapes, the mesh must still be large enough to allow the grapes to fall through. A good balance between these two determining factors has resulted in an average mesh size of about 2.5 centimetres square—just larger than one square inch.

DID YOU  KNOW?

In 2005, Inniskillin Icewine was the top-selling wine product in all duty-free stores around the world—beating out the usual champion, Champagne.

Cold Hard Numbers

In the international market, only Germany comes close to Canada in icewine production, though it is still dwarfed by the Canadian industry. Canada produces between 500,000 and 900,000 litres, or about two million 375-mL bottles, of icewine per year.

Sales of Canadian icewine continue to grow at a rate of 50 percent per year—a staggering pace. Yet the market has not become saturated with the syrupy stuff, because the demand for icewine has grown in tandem with production. The aggressive marketing of Canadian icewine in several Asian countries seems to be successful: Asian markets are particularly thirsty for the frozen nectar.

Cold Hard Counterfeits

The downside of icewine's popularity is that it is being counterfeited on an unprecedented scale, especially in Southeast Asia. According to some reports, in Taiwan, as much as 50 percent of products claiming to be icewine are fakes. For producers selling a large amount of icewine in Asian markets, these figures are more than a little disturbing.

There are ways to prevent buying a counterfeit bottle. First, in Canada, counterfeit icewine is rare. Second, if the bottle bears the VQA (Vintners Quality Alliance) name and symbol, it is guaranteed to be authentic, and this holds true for most of the rest of the world as well. Consumers purchasing Canadian icewine abroad must be more careful with their purchases, but, in general, shopping at a reputable establishment and looking for the VQA symbol are two ways of minimizing the risk.

DID YOU KNOW?

Ontario's Pillitteri Estates Winery exports about 75 percent of its icewine to Asia.

Making the List

In 2008, another milestone in Canadian wine history was marked. For the first time, a Canadian wine made *Wine Spectator*'s

Top 100 list: Konzelmann's 2006 Vidal Icewine from the Niagara Peninsula checked in at wine number 100. For those who are unfamiliar with this list or with *Wine Spectator* magazine, know that both are among the most influential forces in the North American wine industry. *Wine Spectator* publishes hundreds of wine ratings, articles and other information about the industry. Its annual Top 100 list is anticipated by many, and the wines that make it are scooped up quickly.

Although many judge the hype associated with the Top 100 list to be superficial, there's no arguing the power it has over buyers' decisions. Making this list is a big accomplishment for Canada's wine industry as a whole and is just one more sign that Canadian wines are becoming increasingly well known outside our borders.

The Most Expensive Wine in the World

Icewine is certainly not the cheapest wine on the shelves. In fact, the world's most expensive wine is none other than a bottle of Canadian icewine: in 2006, Royal DeMaria released five cases of their 2000 Chardonnay icewine, each 375-mL bottle bearing a price tag of a whopping C$30,000. This makes Bordeaux's famously expensive wines—Petrús, Mouton-Rothschild, Cheval-Blanc—look like bargain-bin bottles.

The icewine is from the Billy Myers Series and takes its name from a local Niagara grape grower. The first buyer was a businessman from Saudi Arabia, and there are reportedly several potential buyers in Japan. Winemaker Joseph DeMaria is pleased (no kidding!) at the response to this wine and has even gone so far as to predict that the last bottle in this series will sell for roughly half a million dollars. (As of press time, only 18 bottles of the icewine remained and were selling for C$250,000!)

Paying that much for a (half!) bottle of wine clearly places the buyer in the realm of status seeker, not wine lover. Many have speculated on how a winery can charge so much and still find buyers; some have even suggested that it's a sham. Whatever the case, I can't resist asking: what if the wine is corked? At that price, I suppose you would drink it anyway.

Why the Price?

Although not all as pricey as Royal DeMaria's six-figure bottles, icewines on average cost more than table wines. Prices usually start at about C$40 for a 375-mL bottle, but it's not uncommon to see bottles going for about C$100. Keep in mind that these are local prices; these bottles go for a lot more abroad.

However, unlike the artificially inflated prices of many wines, icewine's cost is justifiable, to some extent, largely because icewine is one of the riskiest wines to make. If the temperature does not fall below the minimum requirement of −8°C and stay there for a few days without dipping too low or climbing too high, icewine simply cannot be made. Granted, in Canada, this is rarely an issue, but the winemaker is still very much at the mercy of Mother Nature.

Also adding to the price is the high cost of bird netting and labour—although machines are increasingly used for harvest, many icewine grapes are still harvested by hand. Finally, the biggest reason for the high price of icewine is the extremely low yield. By the time icewine grapes are harvested, they have shrivelled up and lost the majority of their water content; the result is that they yield only one or two precious drops of concentrated liquid. Frozen grapes produce less than 20 percent of the volume of juice extracted from regular, unfrozen grapes—that's 80 to 90 percent less than the amount of juice pressed from grapes for dry table wine. On average, one healthy grapevine yields enough juice to make a standard bottle of wine. This same vine, however, will only produce one small glass of icewine.

Refrigerator Wine

Icewine's resounding international popularity has prompted vintners around the world to try their hand at crafting these wines. However, few wine-producing countries have the right climate for regularly making icewine. This hasn't prevented enterprising producers from finding alternative methods of making it. After all, icewine is simply wine made from frozen grapes—and everyone owns a freezer!

Many wineries in various countries have experimented with artificially freezing grapes in large commercial freezers. Even Walter Hainle, during his initial icewine trials in the late 1970s, tried this method—but he was very disappointed with the results and never tried it again. Fortunately, wineries using artificial means to freeze grapes are not allowed to label their products "icewine." This hasn't daunted some producers, however. California's Bonny Doon Vineyard produces a dessert wine from artificially frozen Muscat grapes, which it mischievously calls "Vin de Glacière"—literally, "refrigerator wine."

A Matter of Taste

What does icewine taste like, anyway? What makes it so popular that it can fetch exorbitant prices? For starters, icewine is extremely aromatic, with luscious tropical fruit flavours such as pineapple, mango, guava and grapefruit. The aromas just leap out of the glass, arousing interest in even the most jaded of wine drinkers.

Another fascinating aspect of icewine is its hallmark balance between sweetness and acidity. Icewine is one of the sweetest wines in the world, yet the sugar is held in check by a balancing streak of zesty acidity. The acidity cleanses the palate and leaves you feeling refreshed and ready for another sip. It also makes icewine very food-friendly; it pairs particularly well with a wide variety of desserts—an oenophile's dream!

Wine Popsicles

Long before Walter Hainle made the first icewine, the possibility of using frozen grapes was already being considered in Canada. In a paper from 1866, J.M. de Courtenay, one of the most vocal proponents of the Canadian wine industry in the late 1800s, discussed the potential of what he termed "Essence of Wine."

De Courtenay described this essence as wine "ether" and stated that the only way to obtain it is through freezing, because the water and ether separate when frozen. When a grape is frozen, the water in the berry turns to ice; when it's pressed, only the concentrated juice comes out. This is the basic principle of icewine production.

However, de Courtenay missed the mark slightly with his concept, because he obtained his wine essence from freezing finished wine, not grapes. He also advocated using this essence not for drinking but for strengthening other wines. His predictions for congealed wine were rather grandiose; de Courtenay thought that wine essence would become a great source of national prosperity for Canada, because wines can't freeze reliably in Europe and therefore the demand for frozen Canadian wine would be very high. Although his predictions were off, I'm sure de Courtenay would be pleased to see Canada's success with its icewine.

THE BAD: POP WINES

The Pop World

They are the Coca-Colas of the wine world: "pop" wines are sweet, fizzy and, above all, cheap. Pop wines take their name from the sound of the bottle being opened—but, although a merrily popping cork certainly sounds cheery, in the case of pop wines, it's also rather ominous. Indeed, pop heralded a new age of Canadian wine. Throughout the 1970s, pop wines ruled the market. Baby boomers raised on soft drinks were the targeted consumer of these wines—and they couldn't get enough of them. Most pop wines were mass-produced and often made from low-quality, native Canadian grapes. Mostly unsuitable for good table wine, they were just fine for the pop wine industry— all that added sugar and carbonation masked any off-putting aromas and flavours.

Leader of the Pops

The unquestioned leader of Canada's pop wines was Baby Duck, which you can still buy. In the 1970s, Baby Duck was the most popular wine in Canada—a title it held for several years. It has been estimated that, out of every 24 bottles of wine sold during the '70s, at least one was Baby Duck.

DID YOU KNOW?

In 1978, Canadians consumed eight million bottles of Baby Duck.

True Canadians?

Baby Duck and a host of other pop wines were so common throughout the country that, during the 1970s, they became

synonymous with Canadian wines as a whole. Although plenty of other wines were being made in a wide variety of styles, they were largely overshadowed by Baby Duck and its ilk. Pop wines truly dominated the industry; producers in Ontario and British Columbia bought thousands of tonnes of grapes and pumped out an inordinate amount of sweet, fizzy juice.

Although pop wines certainly brought in plenty of cash for producers and grape growers, they worked against the Canadian wine industry's efforts to establish a credible international reputation. On the plus side, there's no denying that pop wines did get a generation of people who normally drank beer or spirits to drink wine.

Cold Duck

Baby Duck wasn't the first pop wine, though it certainly galvanized the trend. In the 1960s and '70s, a huge marketing campaign in the United States aimed to convert beer and soda drinkers into wine drinkers through the introduction of sweet, low-alcohol, carbonated "wine." The campaign was spearheaded by a brand of pop wine called Cold Duck. Cold Duck was named for a German tradition: at the end of a party, all the wines are combined in a single bowl and called the "cold end." Because the German word for end (*ende*) and duck (*ente*) are similar, the name Cold Duck was born. (The tradition isn't clear about whether or not anyone has to actually drink this mixture.)

DID YOU KNOW?

Cold Duck was invented by Harold Borgman, owner of Detroit's Pontchartrain Wine Cellars, in 1937.

Birth of the Baby

Baby Duck was a direct emulation of Cold Duck. The infamous Baby was the creation of British Columbia's Andrés Wines. Before launching Baby Duck, Andrés had introduced a few other pop wines. The first was released in the mid-1960s, just after pop wine took flight in the United States. Others, both reds and whites, followed. Then, in 1971, Baby Duck was born.

The success was immediate and enduring. Sales of Baby Duck skyrocketed, and many other wineries in British Columbia and Ontario scrambled to put out their own version of the wine. Throughout the 1970s, a veritable zoo was available for sale at liquor stores: Cool Duck, Fuddle Duck, Cold Turkey, Baby Bear and Pink Flamingo.

 **Andrés Wines**

Andrés Wines was founded by Andrew Peller in 1961 in Port Moody, British Columbia. The winery still exists—in fact, it is the largest domestically owned wine company in Canada. The early success of the winery was based on Baby Duck and a host of other pop wines released throughout the 1960s and 1970s; indeed, the winery's name became almost synonymous with its most popular product.

Andrés attained immediate success in BC, to such a degree that Peller founded a sister winery in Ontario in 1969. He had also established bottling plants across Canada by 1974. In 1968, Peller spearheaded the development of Inkameep Vineyards in the Okanagan, BC's first large-scale planting of Vitis vinifera grape varieties. Along with Baby Duck, Andrés

Winery Profile

offers several high-end labels, including Hillebrand, Thirty Bench, Sandhill, Red Rooster and Peller Estates, which recently gained a brand-new, state-of-the-art winery in Niagara.

Not Just an Innocent Bird

The huge success of Baby Duck and the rest of Canada's pop wines had an equally huge impact on Canada's wine industry. To keep up with the demand of its rabid followers, Andrés had to buy unprecedented amounts of grapes. Baby Duck was initially made from Canada's native *Vitis labrusca* varieties; although these grapes didn't make palatable dry wines, thanks to their off-putting musky, or "foxy," aroma, they were prefect for pop wine because the carbonation and sugar hid the foxiness. *Labrusca* varieties are also high yielding, which only encouraged BC grape growers to continue cultivating them—impeding the growth of better-quality *vinifera* grapes.

When local growers couldn't keep up with Andrés' insatiable demand for grapes, the winery began importing fruit from California. Grapes from California were cheap—sometimes cheaper than local grapes, leaving BC grape growers facing a huge potential loss in revenue. In 1970, the growers formed the Grape Growers Marketing Board in conjunction with the BC government to protect the local industry. The Board negotiated purchasing contracts with BC's grape growers, ensuring that none of the crop went unsold. Although the policy certainly helped growers, it also effectively lowered their accountability to zero; their crops would be sold, regardless of their condition or quality.

Taste Buds Grow Up

Despite pop wine's immense popularity and its ramifications on the industry, Canadian vineyards are now dominated by the lower-yielding, fragile, expensive *vinifera* varieties. Indeed, for many years, producing dry, premium table wines seemed only the dream of a few isolated romantics. Pop wines continued to reign throughout the 1970s, and real changes weren't made to the industry until the end of the decade. Fortunately, that old adage—all things must come to an end—holds true even in the wine world. The palates of wine drinkers began to "grow up," and many consumers switched to dry table wines. Slowly but surely, market shares of pop wines began to decline, as sales of table wines rose.

DID YOU KNOW?

In 1980, Andrés demoted Baby Duck from a wine to a "refreshment beverage."

Modern Ducks

Although pop wines have never attained the same degree of popularity since their heyday in the 1970s, a few modern versions of these wines, including Baby Duck, can still be found in Canadian liquor stores. However, also gracing the shelves are several brands of wine coolers, which are made in a style similar to those original pop wines—sweet, fizzy and low in alcohol. The difference is that these products are clearly labelled as wine coolers or wine beverages and are not intended to pass for "real" wine. Also, wine coolers make up a relatively small percentage of wine products sold in Canada—proof that most Canadians have changed their palates considerably and no longer prefer sweet, fizzy kid's juice.

A Sparkling Future

For those who lived through the pop-wine era, the mention of anything that's bubbly and made in Canada (unless it's beer, of course) will probably elicit an involuntary grimace. But Canadian sparkling wine has come a long way since those days; it's possible that bubbly could become the industry's next icewine, in terms of both quality and worldwide recognition. A new generation of wine lovers has come of age—too young to have experienced pop wines at their peak, they're less prejudiced about Canada's current effervescent offerings.

Grapes destined for sparkling wines differ from still wines in one distinct way: they need to have high acidity—even to the point of being slightly unripe. This is why the Champagne region is so successful with its bubblies; as the most northern wine region in France, the area produces grapes that rarely achieve full ripeness and are quite acidic and tart—perfect for making sparkling wine.

Like the Champagne region, Nova Scotia and Québec grow grapes that often do not fully ripen in their cool climates, but these grapes work very well for bubbly, and sparkling wines from these areas are quickly gaining a reputation for being high in quality and a superb value, compared to their French counterpart. Québec producers have already seen success with their sparkling cider and sparkling ice cider, and it will only be a matter of time before they gain recognition for sparkling grape wines. Expect to see more bubbly from all regions of Canada, including the Atlantic provinces, gracing liquor-store shelves across the country.

THE SHADY: PSEUDO LABELS AND MORE

Pseudo Labels

Throughout the 1970s and 1980s, many of Canada's wines were marketed under so-called pseudo labels, which employed foreign language and terminology to help sell them. These labels equated the wine with a European counterpart, imbuing it with false authenticity and quality. They were also intended to combat the rising popularity of imported wine. Europe was (and still is, by many accounts) seen as a bastion of culture, especially wine culture, and, by making these wines seem more European, they instantly became popular.

Schloss Laderheim

The first example of a pseudo label came in 1977, with Calona's release of Schloss Laderheim. The word *schloss*, which is commonly found on German wine labels, means "castle," though when used on wine labels, it usually means "estate grown"— grapes used to make the wine came exclusively from a particular estate. Schloss Laderheim is an off-dry white wine, very similar in style to the average German wine, which was popular at the time. The success of this wine spawned several similar pseudo labels from other wineries, such as Andrés' Hochtaler.

Sprechen Sie Deutsch?

During the late 1970s and continuing into the 1980s, liquor store shelves were littered with such faux-European names as Barbarosso, Alpenweiss, Toscano and Klosterberg. Although the names might have sounded authentic (at least to the uninitiated), they were entirely made up. However, they were similar enough to the actual European names that many European producers threatened to sue. For example, Calona's Schloss Laderheim wine prompted several German producers to try taking Calona to court, but the winery managed to narrowly avoid this unpleasant fate. Ultimately, a case couldn't be made against any of these wines, because the names technically did not have any European precedent.

DID YOU  KNOW?

You can still buy Schloss Laderheim, along with several other pseudo labels, such as Hochtaler and Toscano.

Canadian Liebfraumilch

By the time pseudo labels hit the Canadian wine scene, several producers had already been using actual European terminology on their labels. In 1965, Growers' Wine Company in British Columbia released "Canadian Liebfraumilch." A semisweet style of German white wine, Liebfraumilch was popular during the 1960s and 1970s, and most people know it by its most popular North American incarnations, Blue Nun and Black Tower.

Growers' Liebfraumilch was obviously not authentic, but many consumers purchased it because of its authentic name. It wasn't long, however, before Growers' was faced with a lawsuit from seven German wineries over the use of the name. The company settled the matter quickly to avoid bad publicity, renaming the wine Rhine Castle. Growers' also tried to release a red wine called Beaujolais, but its name was changed to Beau Séjour, for Calona's vineyard at Okanagan Mission, before the wine made it to store shelves.

DID YOU KNOW?

The literal translation of Liebfraumilch is "beloved lady's milk."

Canadian Sherry

One Canadian producer, Château-Gai, got into trouble for labelling its fortified wines as "sherry." Strangely enough, the company ran into difficulties with the British, not the Spanish. Although true sherry comes from the Jerez region of Spain, most of the shippers are British, and they objected to Château-Gai's appropriation of their livelihood for the winery's own gain. Luckily, the matter was resolved fairly quickly. In Britain, Château-Gai's sherry became known as Ontario Cream Appetizer, Solera Canadian Appetizer and Dry Canadian Appetizer.

Will the Real Champagne Please Stand Up

The most persistently misused European name on Canadian wine labels—and likely on those of many other countries, as well—is the term Champagne. Also one of the most misunderstood terms in the wine world, "Champagne" is, for many consumers, especially non-Europeans, taken as a generic term for sparkling wine. However, in reality, Champagne is the name of the region in France that produces sparkling wine; French wines are commonly referred to by the name of their place of origin. Because the bubblies from Champagne became so well known throughout the world, it became a common trend to mistakenly refer to all sparkling wines by this name. Champagne producers have been fighting this uphill battle for decades, and although Champagne producers are (in)famous for taking people to court for misuse of the term, you can't wholly condemn them—they're trying to protect their heritage.

DID YOU  KNOW?

The first example of Canadian producers hijacking the Champagne name dates back to 1894, when J.S. Hamilton's Pelee Island winery released a sparkling wine named L'Empereur Champagne.

Don't Call it Champagne

Most countries have either passed a law or signed an agreement restricting the use of the term Champagne. Legally, it can only be used on bottles originating within the specifically delineated region of Champagne in France. This holds true for the entirety of the wine label and not just the name; producers outside the region are not allowed to make any reference to Champagne or the Méthode Champenoise, which refers to a specific method of making Champagne in this region. Although anyone can make wine in this method, it cannot be mentioned on the label. Other terms, most commonly "traditional method," are used instead.

Losing the Label

Canadian producers have used the term Champagne on labels for decades. But, as fate would have it, only one, Niagara's Château-Gai, was singled out and taken to court. In 1964, the L'Institut National des Appellations d'Origine des Vins et Eaux-de-Vie (the governing body in France that regulates the Appellation d'Origine Contrôlée, or AOC, France's wine-appellation classification system) and 15 companies in the Champagne region sought damages and an injunction forbidding the use of the word "Champagne." This costly legal battle lasted for a decade. Finally, in 1974, the Canadian court ruled in favour of the French. The basis of the French victory was a 1933 trade agreement between Canada and France. However, this ruling only applied in Québec, and the Canadian government stepped in before another decade-long round of litigation could begin in other provinces; the trade agreement was abrogated in December 1977.

Champagne Fakery

In 1984, French Champagne producers took seven Ontario wineries to court for using the words "Canadian Champagne" on their labels. However, this time, they were not victorious. After another lengthy battle, the Canadian court ruled against the French, arguing that they had waited too long to bring the action—and that nobody would mistake Canadian Champagne for the real thing, anyway. This is perhaps a testament to the real state of affairs: products requiring the crutch of famous wine nomenclature are almost certainly not products that can stand up to scrutiny on their own. They are cheap, mass-produced wines that appeal to those without much interest or knowledge of wine. Although using the word Champagne on the label certainly helped sell bottles, it did nothing to improve the reputation of Canada's wines.

Thankfully, the vast majority of Canadian wines no longer use any kind of European terminology or pseudo labels.

Making the Change

In 2003, Canada signed an agreement to begin phasing out the use of European names and terms on wine labels, including Champagne. As of December 31, 2013, Canadian wine producers will no longer be able to use the word Champagne, nor the words Port, Sherry or Chablis.

DID YOU  KNOW?

Although the rest of the industry stopped marketing wines as Champagne, as of 2009, some producers were still using the term on their labels. Andrés Winery, for example, still sells a product called Baby Canadian Champagne.

ONTARIO: A YOUTHFUL OLD INDUSTRY

Growing on the Great Lakes

Ontario is home to more than 100 grape wine producers and more than 40 producers of fruit wines. The vast majority are located in the Niagara region, which wraps around the south-eastern end of Lake Ontario. Although not technically the first wine region in Canada, Niagara is the largest and is the first in which most of the major winemaking advancements occurred. Wine is also made in the much smaller regions of Lake Erie North Shore, which hugs the northern shoreline of the Great Lake in a curve extending from the mouth of the Detroit River to Ridgetown, and Prince Edward County, an island just off the north shore of Lake Ontario midway between Toronto and Kingston. Wine is even made in and around the Greater Toronto Area.

DID YOU KNOW?

More than two-thirds of Ontario's wineries opened after 1999.

Critical Condemnations

Ontario's wine industry has come a long way in three decades. In 1972, world-renowned wine critic Hugh Johnson made the following comments about Ontario wines: "The foulness of taste is what I remember best—an artificial, scented, soapy flavour."

Similarly, Henry Gibson (a reputed satirist and wine connoisseur) is quoted in a 1975 issue of *Foodservice and Hospitality* as saying: "Ontario wines? Hah!! I wouldn't even wash my car with them."

Canada's own wine critic, Tony Aspler, also sided against Ontario's early wines. In his 1997 book, *Travels with my Corkscrew*, Aspler notes that, for years, a sort of reverse psychology applied to Canadian wines: "Anything that bore an imported label had to be better than the local article. You were lucky if you could find an Ontario wine on a Toronto wine list."

DID YOU KNOW?

Although the Canadian province of Ontario wasn't mentioned once in the first edition of Hugh Johnson's *World Atlas of Wine*, the community of Ontario, California, was.

LCBOh-Oh

The LCBO—the Liquor Control Board of Ontario—was born when the Ontario government introduced the Liquor Control Act in 1927. A government monopoly, the LCBO purchased all alcoholic beverages for the entire province and

was set up to regulate the sale of wine and other types of alcohol. Alcoholic beverages could only be sold in the province's government-run stores. The vast majority of alcoholic beverages are still sold through LCBO stores, but you can also buy wine from a small number of privately owned specialty wine stores, such as the Wine Rack stores owned by Vincor International, and the Vineyards Estate Wines stores, owned by Andrés Wines.

DID YOU KNOW?

In Ontario, government taxes comprise approximately 70 percent of the price of a bottle of wine. Ouch!

A Trip to the LCBO in 1976

LCBO stores are like warehouses—they are huge, holding thousands of different products to service thousands of people in the neighbouring communities. However, as you might expect, they don't have the greatest ambience. This amusing description, appearing in Tony Aspler's book, *Travels with my Corkscrew*, documents the process of buying wine in an Ontario LCBO store:

"You had to consult what looked like a railway time table for a list of available products, write down the wine and the product number, your name and address. Then you had to take your docket to the counter where you presented it to some surly fellow who looked as if he'd rather be bowling. He would disappear into the back and emerge with a brown paper bag. He would slip it down surreptitiously to give you a look at the label and then cover it again, for all the world as if he were selling you a girlie magazine."

DID YOU  KNOW?

The LCBO is the world's largest single purchaser of wine, buying 8.5 million cases each year.

Thinking Outside the Box (Store)

Wine buyers in Ontario now have alternatives to the LCBO. The Wine Rack and Vineyards Estate Wines boutique wine stores operate throughout the province, allowing consumers to browse through shelves of bottles before making their purchases. Most wineries also have retail stores or offer bottles for sale on-site, and many offer online shopping, even delivering the wine to your house if you live in the area.

The Big Six

The LCBO's efforts to regulate both wine production and public consumption resulted in the consolidation of the industry. During the 1920s and '30s, surviving wineries bought out those that had gone bankrupt—or were about to—for very low sums, usually between $5000 and $10,000 each. In just a few short years, the number of wineries in Ontario was reduced from 61 to eight. No new licences were granted until 1975, almost half a century later.

Out of the eight remaining wineries, only six survived. Some have termed these the Big Six, because they dominated Ontario's wine industry for so long (some of them still do). The Big Six are Barnes, Brights, Château-Gai, Jordan, London and Andrés. These six wineries dominated the industry until the mid-1970s and produced wines that were sweet and high in alcohol content, to meet the demand for fortified wines, which were popular during the 1950s and 1960s.

To Boldly Go...

Inniskillin Wines received its licence on July 5, 1975; the Podamer Champagne Company followed a few months later. The two young wineries were faced with the daunting task of competing with the Big Six—and they rose to the challenge. Inniskillin was instrumental in setting the trend for the next phase of Ontario's wine industry—its goal was to produce wines made from 100-percent locally grown grapes, preferably *vinifera* varieties. The popularity of this wine forced the Big Six to revamp their own portfolios.

Growing Their Own

Although a number of Ontario's large wine companies had once owned their own vineyards, their vines had been sold off in favour of purchased grapes. Inniskillin's decision to use its own grapes set off a chain reaction that saw the acquisition of vineyards by the large producers and the formation of several estate wineries. These estate wineries were usually much smaller, producing wines from vineyards under their ownership and/or control. Through their combined critical mass, these small wineries began reshaping the Ontario wine industry, forcing the large wineries to adopt similar methods.

The Big Six Scramble

In the face of the young upstart wineries that had begun snapping up awards and eating into their market revenue, the Big Six undertook a series of changes and consolidations in an attempt to regain their lost revenue. Many expanded into other provinces, mainly British Columbia; others consolidated their power through buyouts: Brights purchased Jordan, and Château-Gai bought Barnes. This latter buyout was a precursor to the establishment of the largest wine company in Canada, Vincor.

Conglomerate Wine

Vincor International, which was established in 1993 by the merger of Cartier-Inniskillin with Brights, can trace its history back to the late 1800s, with the inception of Brights. Brights was established in 1874 as the Niagara Falls Wine Company. It changed its name to T.G. Bright & Company in 1911. Over the course of the next century, Brights went on to acquire Jordan, St. Michelle Cellars and Cartier Wines-Inniskillin.

In 2006, Vincor was acquired by Constellation Brands, the largest wine company in the world; Vincor operates as a division under Constellation. Vincor has more than a dozen labels under its banner, many of which are household names in Canada: Inniskillin, Sawmill Creek, Jackson-Triggs, Sumac Ridge, Hawthorne Mountain Vineyards, Osoyoos Larose and Le Clos Jordanne. Vincor also owns wineries in Québec, New Brunswick, California, Washington, Australia, New Zealand and the United Kingdom.

The Free Trade Pullout Program

The 1989 Free Trade Agreement (FTA) with the United States took its toll on Canada's wine industry, by lifting the economic barriers that had protected Canadian wines and putting the nation's wines at the mercy of the open market. At the time, California's wines were far superior in quality to Canada's offerings—in an open market, Canadian wines would face a huge loss in revenue to the American producers.

To help the industry compete with the better-quality American wines, and to prevent California wines from dominating wine sales in Canada, the government introduced a pullout program that resulted in more than half of Ontario's *labrusca* vines being replaced by *vinifera* varieties. In just one year, the province's wine production dropped to a fraction of its former output. Yet, extreme as it was, the pullout program forced producers to start making better-quality wines; this single incident changed the face of the Canadian wine industry.

DID YOU KNOW?

In less than two years, Ontario lost almost half its acreage of wine grapes, dropping to 3200 hectares from 6000.

An Appellation of Our Own

Establishing the Vintners Quality Alliance (VQA) was an extremely important development in Ontario's wine industry. The VQA is Canada's appellation system, akin to France's Appellation d'Origine Controlée (AOC). This provincially run legislating body was launched in 1988 to ensure the quality of Ontario's wines by setting standards and requirements. All wines bearing the VQA logo must meet these quality requirements and must also be submitted to a tasting panel; these standards are enforced by the Vintners Quality Alliance Ontario. Although not all Ontario wines are VQA certified, a good percentage are. The VQA logo is the single best identifier of a high-quality product.

DID YOU KNOW?

More than 85 percent of Ontario's wines are VQA certified.

Divvying it Up

In 2004, the VQA announced the establishment of 11 sub-appellations of the Niagara Peninsula, which was then the largest appellation in Ontario. The idea was to differentiate the varying soils and *terroir* (see Wine 101, page 198) of each particular zone; in France and the rest of the Old World, appellations are not so much political as they are agricultural. Developments such as these are signposts that mark the continued growth and maturation of the wine industry. As Ontario continues to experiment with different grapes, regions and production techniques, it will further establish and refine its own niche in the wine world, creating new regions based on the distinct differences marking each unique grape-growing area.

DID YOU KNOW?

As of 2008, Ontario's top varieties of white-wine grapes (in terms of vineyard space) are Vidal (used primarily for icewine), Chardonnay and Riesling. The top red varieties are Cabernet Franc, Merlot and Cabernet Sauvignon.

BRITISH COLUMBIA: CANADA'S PRODIGY PROVINCE

Valley Vines

British Columbia boasts more than 120 wineries, including dozens of fruit wineries. More than two-thirds of them are located in the Okanagan Valley. The area has a long history of growing tree fruit in addition to grapes, which is partly why the Okanagan has the highest concentration of fruit wineries in Canada. However, with the soaring profitability of grape growing, more and more orchardists have pulled up their trees and planted vines.

DID YOU KNOW?

British Columbia has an estimated 3680 hectares of grape vines, up from just 400 hectares planted in 1989.

Playing Catch-up

British Columbia's wine industry got started somewhat later than Ontario's; this should come as no surprise, given its distance from the eastern part of the country, which was settled first. Although the province's wine industry has made up for lost time, it is still a young industry, even by Canadian standards. Most vines were planted after 1990, and wine has only really been made there for three generations. The industry's youth is partly the reason the region is so paradoxical; you can find wildly different grape varieties growing side by side—something that just doesn't happen in Europe, where the grapes best suited to each area have been grown for centuries.

DID YOU  KNOW?

It is believed that some of the oldest grape vines in the Okanagan are located in CedarCreek's vineyards. The Merlot vines were planted in the 1970s.

Vine Pioneer

The first vineyard devoted to wine grapes was not developed in British Columbia until 1928. The pioneer behind this vineyard, horticulturist J.W. Hughes, bought 18 hectares in Kelowna and planted locally propagated vines. Hughes planted several grape varieties, to see which would fare best in the Okanagan's climate. All the varieties belonged to Canada's native *Vitis labrusca* species; at the time it was thought that Canada's climate was too harsh for *Vitis vinifera* grapes. The vineyard did so well that, four years later, Hughes signed a contract with BC's Growers' Wine Company. His grapes were trucked all the way to the Growers' cooperative on Vancouver Island, where they were made into wine.

Grape Trials

The Summerland Research Station (originally called the Dominion Experimental Station), a federal government agricultural research station, was established in 1914 on the west side of Lake Okanagan. In 1928, the station began the first of its trials of grape varieties, to determine which grapes were best suited to British Columbia's climate. By 1936, almost 150 grape varieties were being tested, the vast majority of which were *labrusca*. The program was halted in 1948, however, because of a lack of interest; British Columbia only had two main wineries at the time, Growers' and Calona.

Grape trials weren't resumed until 1957, when renewed interest in the BC wine industry was spurred by the opening of two new wineries in Vancouver suburbs: Pacific Western Wines in 1959 and Andrés Wines in 1961. This second round of trials focused on several hybrid varieties brought in from Ontario. Research continued until 1995, when Agriculture Canada's budget cuts eliminated the viticulture program.

Not So Okay

Calona Wines Limited was established in 1932 to make apple wine. In the years before the winery opened, a series of abundant harvests flooded the market with apples. The common lament was "a cent a pound or on the ground"—there were so many apples, they literally rotted on the trees. Prices plummeted, and many farmers were forced to tear out their orchards and plant grapes, which were far more profitable. Calona took advantage of the plummeting apple prices to make apple wine and other fruit-based products, from brandy to tomato juice.

The company was founded by Giuseppe Ghezzi, an Italian immigrant; W.A.C. Bennett, a local hardware store owner; and Pasquale "Cap" Capozzi, an Italian grocer, under the uninspiring name of Domestic Wines and By-Products. Despite the Depression, the trio managed to scrape together enough funds to get started and release their first product lineup, consisting of four apple-based wines: Okay Red, Okay Clear, Okay Port and Okay Champagne. The name is a bit of a misnomer, however, because these wines were reputedly far from "okay." Poorly made, many refermented on the shelves. Sales were disastrous, especially against the prosperous Growers' wines. With no market for apple wines, the company shifted focus, changed its name and began producing wines using grapes from California. Because California grapes were superior in quality to the local produce, Calona gained a measure of security and prosperity.

DID YOU  KNOW?

Calona's name derives from the phonetic spelling of the aboriginal place name of the company's location: Kelowna.

Calona's Holy Lifeline

Canada's sacramental wine was being imported from Europe even into the 1900s. Things changed in 1936, however, when Father W.B. McKenzie, a priest from Kelowna, saw the plentiful supply of local wine (and the need to spur local economy during the Depression) and approached the Archbishop of Vancouver with the suggestion that the Catholic Church replace its imported sacramental wine with local products.

McKenzie had the Calona winery in mind to receive this boon, and the winery sent a sample of wine, along with a $45 fee, to Dr. Georges Baril at the Université de Montréal. Baril analyzed the wine (there's no mention of what he did with the fee) and pronounced it canonically acceptable—that is, it was made from natural ingredients and therefore fit for use by the church. The wine also weighed in at a hefty 14.97 percent alcohol—quite high for current standards but relatively light-weight in that era of fortified wines. Shortly afterward, Calona signed a contract with the church, agreeing to produce sacramental wine. The contract was a blessing; these sacramental wines, bottled under the St. John brand, proved to be Calona's lifeline during the difficult years of the Depression.

Friends in High Places

W.A.C. Bennett, one of the founders of Calona Wines, left the wine business in 1940 to pursue a career in politics and became premier of British Columbia in 1952. However, he kept wine in the forefront of his life and was instrumental in implementing legislation that changed the face of the indus-try and promoted BC as a grape-growing province. In 1960, the government passed a law requiring wines vinified in the province to contain a minimum percentage of local fruit. Initially set at 25 percent, the minimum rose to 50 percent in 1962 and 65 percent in 1965.

DID YOU KNOW?

Despite being heavily involved in the BC wine industry, W.A.C. Bennett was a teetotaller.

New Faces

BC's legislative changes marked the beginning of the first concerted growth of the province's wine industry. Two winer-ies opened in 1966, both in the Okanagan: Casabello (which no longer exists) and Mission Hill. Calona and Growers' also experienced a marked increase in sales at the time. Plantings sprang up all over, with annual wine grape production in the 1970s rising to 10,200 tonnes from 2140 tonnes in the 1960s.

Breeding Grapes

One of the most important developments in the BC wine industry was the Becker Project, an eight-year trial of European grape varieties that began in 1977. The project was headed by Dr. Helmut Becker, the director of grape breeding at Geisenheim, a leading German wine university. The vines were planted in test plots near Kelowna and Oliver, and the grapes were made into wine at the Summerland Research Station. The Becker Project was instrumental in proving that *vinifera* varieties could indeed grow in BC's climate; it also helped determine which of these varieties would perform the best. It was the first step in Canada's vineyard overhaul, in which the native *labrusca* varieties were replaced by the better-quality European grapes.

DID YOU  KNOW?

As of 2008, the top varieties of white-wine grapes in BC (in terms of vineyard space) were Pinot Gris, Chardonnay, Gewurztraminer and Sauvignon Blanc. The top red varieties were Merlot, Pinot Noir, Cabernet Sauvignon and Syrah.

Grape Estates
In 1978, the BC government passed the estate winery licence, modelled on California's estate winery system. At the time, none of the province's wineries owned their own vineyards; grapes were purchased from growers. The quality of these grapes was low, however, largely because of the efforts of the Grape Growers Marketing Board, which was formed in 1970 to "protect" the local industry when BC's wineries began buying grapes from California, sometimes for less than the local produce. Worried that they might soon be out of a livelihood, the growers formed the Board to ensure that their grapes would find buyers. In conjunction with the BC government, the Board negotiated contracts between growers and buyers, ensuring that all the locally grown grapes were sold before wineries could bring in foreign grapes.

Although the program ensured financial profitability, the quality of the grapes—and of the resulting wines—took a nosedive. Because the sale of their crops was guaranteed even before they had been harvested, growers didn't need to spend the extra time and effort required to produce quality crops—so they didn't.

At the time, California's wines were just beginning to take the world by storm. To compete with the California product and raise the quality of local wines, the BC government created the estate winery licence, which required each estate winery to own or control a minimum of eight hectares of vineyard. The premise was that producers would make better wines from their own vineyards.

The estate winery program was not a blanket success; of the original five, only two estate wineries succeeded: Gray Monk and Sumac Ridge. The reason for this was, ultimately, quality—both wineries primarily used *vinifera* grapes and thus made better wines.

Making It Simple

By the mid-1990s, British Columbia had a three-tiered winery system. Farm wineries, at the bottom of the pile, were required to own a minimum of 1.6 hectares of vines and were limited to producing 37,800 litres of wine a year made solely from BC grapes. Estate wineries rode the middle ground; they had to own at least eight hectares of vines and could produce up to 151,000 litres of wine, also only from BC grapes. Major wineries, which produced any amount over the limit set for estate wineries, were not required to own their own vineyards and could produce local wines and wines made from a blend of imported and local grapes. In 1998, the BC government decided to simplify things and established a new licensing policy that effectively created one licence for all wineries.

DID YOU KNOW?

A phenomenon known as bulldozer disease has affected some of BC's newer vineyards. When the land has been ineptly contoured by heavy equipment—mixing the soil layers and burying the topsoil—vines grow poorly.

Winery Profile — Gray Monk Estate Winery

Gray Monk is one of BC's original five estate wineries. Owned and operated by George and Trudy Heiss, the vineyard was planted in 1972 on a steep slope on the west side of Lake Okanagan. The Heisses are Okanagan wine pioneers who planted experimental varieties over the following decades to determine which grapes would grow and flourish in this new wine region. Their first vines comprised 33 German varieties, including Pinot Gris, which is known as Gray Monk in Austria, George's birthplace. Gray Monk's Pinot Gris has become the winery's flagship wine as well as its namesake.

The Heisses' efforts paid off; in 1978, they were given vine cuttings from Helmut Becker of Germany's prestigious wine university, the Geisenheim Institute. The plantings were part of the Becker Project, an eight-year intensive trial of *vinifera* varieties in Canada. From these formative beginnings, Gray Monk quickly emerged as an industry leader with an impressive portfolio of several dozen wines.

Setting Standards

In 1990, British Columbia launched the Vintners Quality Alliance (VQA) system, based on the VQA established by Ontario two years earlier. The VQA ensures the quality of British Columbia's wines by setting and enforcing various quality standards. For example, all VQA wines must be made from 100-percent-BC-grown grapes and must be submitted to a tasting panel before being sold commercially. These standards are enforced by the British Columbia Wine Institute.

Free Trade and Beyond

Although Canada's entire wine industry was overhauled because of the Free Trade Agreement with the United States, British Columbia was particularly draconian in its transformation; more than two-thirds of the vineyards—mostly those growing *labrusca* and hybrid varieties—were pulled up. In 1989, the harvest dropped to 3840 tonnes from 18,397 tonnes in 1988. Although the upheaval was a huge setback, it was also a huge step forward. Most vineyards were replanted with *vinifera* varieties, which produced better wines than those made from native grapes.

DID YOU  KNOW?

After the 1988 harvest, 110 of 200 growers in British Columbia accepted compensation payments in exchange for pulling up inferior vines and planting *vinifera* wine grapes.

QUÉBEC: COLD-WEATHER WINES

Valiant Vintners
Québec's roughly 40 wineries are nestled in five regions throughout the southern part of the province. Considering that this area regularly experiences winter temperatures of –30°C and lower, the number of valiant winemakers plying their craft here is surprising. A few isolated areas with more favourable microclimates allow ardent growers to successfully grow hardy varieties.

DID YOU KNOW?

Because of the rigours involved in grape growing in Québec, most wineries are boutique operations, making only a few hundred cases of wine per year.

Home Winemakers Lead the Way
The first modern wines made in Québec came from the basements of a few dedicated home winemakers. The first to make wine on a serious scale was Vincent Geloso, an Italian immigrant from Naples. He began importing grapes from California in 1961 and did so well that, five years later, he was granted Québec's first licence for making wine. However, though Geloso was certainly an entrepreneur, his wines did not fare well. Excessive handling of the grapes during the long journey from California resulted in wines that were often oxidized and unpleasant tasting. Undaunted, Geloso helped sponsor a trial of grapevines at Macdonald College in Montréal. However, out of all the grapes planted—mostly French hybrids and a few Italian varieties—none did well enough to be considered for commercial use.

It's a Long Way to…Québec?

By the end of the 1970s, Québec had 11 licensed wineries. None of them owned vineyards, however; all their grapes were imported from other growing regions, such as Niagara and California. Most of the resulting wines were mediocre, because provincial law at the time required wineries to ferment 70 percent of the wine within the province's borders. Québec's lack of proximity to any main wine regions meant that the grapes were often damaged during the lengthy shipping process, and the grape juice fermented on the way—by the time they reached the wineries, they had already oxidized.

DID YOU KNOW?

Québec wines rose in quality in 1978, thanks to the passing of new legislation that allowed Québec vintners to import bulk wine and bottle it in Québec.

A Boutique Operation

Québec's wine industry didn't really take off until the 1980s. Most of the 1970s-era wineries had either closed or merged with large commercial enterprises, leaving behind an industry composed primarily of boutique producers. Québec's first modern vineyard was planted by Christian Barthomeuf, a native of southern France, in 1979. He planted Pinot Noir, Maréchal Foch and Seyval Blanc, but only the Foch and Seyval survived the winter. Barthomeuf's vineyard now provides grapes for the Domaine des Côtes d'Ardoise winery. In 1982, another immigrant from the south of France, Charles-Henri de Coussergues, planted a large vineyard just down the road from Barthomeuf; it went on to become Vignoble de l'Orpailleur. With 200 hectares of vines in production, Québec's wine industry is small in comparison with Canada's other wine regions.

Winterkill

Canada's cold winters are hard on the wine industry and limit the varieties of grapes that can be grown in this country. In Québec, however, winter dwarfs all else. *Vitis vinifera* and many French hybrid varieties can't survive when the mercury dips lower than –25°C—and this happens all winter long in Québec. A few experimental plots of *vinifera* exist, but nothing is grown in significant numbers.

DID YOU  KNOW?

To ensure that their grapes ripen fully, Québec vintners must lower their yields. Because of the province's short growing season, grapes often do not have enough time to fully ripen. Removing some of the young bunches of grapes allows the vine to put more energy into the remaining bunches, improving their chances of reaching full ripeness. The average yield in France is about four bottles of wine per vine; in Québec, each vine yields only a single bottle.

Winter Grapes

Québec wine producers must grow varieties that can withstand very cold temperatures, such as Frontenac, Sabrevois, Ste-Croix and Vandal-Cliche. Most people have probably never heard of these grapes, for good reason—very few are, and have ever been, grown outside of Québec. Most are hybrid varieties that have been developed to withstand the cold while retaining desirable flavour characteristics.

Most Québec wines can taste decidedly foreign to many palates. The wines tend to be lean and tart, because of the short grape-growing season. Yet these wines are invariably unique and can make good food wines when paired with carefully chosen dishes. In general, Québec's white wines fare much better than its reds, which is somewhat unfortunate, given that both local and international wine drinkers tend to prefer red wines. However, the reds are still interesting enough to pique the curiosity of even the most standoffish taster.

DID YOU  KNOW?

The most widely planted grape variety in Québec is Seyval Blanc, a French hybrid.

Survival Tactics

Growing winter-hardy varieties is only one way to ensure that a Québec vineyard survives the winter, and many techniques are employed to keep the vines safe in the cold. One of the most common is "hilling up," first used in Québec in 1982, by oenologist Hervé Durand. Durand got the idea after visiting vineyards using this technique in Russia and China.

Hilling up is just as it sounds—the vines are covered with earth in late autumn. The canes (branches) are lowered on their trellis wires, and the rows are then back-plowed, throwing earth onto the vines and covering their trunks and lower canes. The vines are then uncovered in the spring. Hilling up is the most effective method of winter protection available to the cold-weather winemaker. Unfortunately, it also comes with a high price tag, requiring a yearly investment of several thousand dollars for labour and equipment.

Because hilling up is so pricey and labour-intensive, many growers have experimented with other methods of winter protection, especially in rocky areas or terraced vineyards, where hilling up is impossible. Some success has been met by covering the vines with straw or heavy fabric. Others have tented plastic sheets over the vines, creating a greenhouse-like environment that retains heat, while preventing frost from settling on the vines. However, none of these techniques works as well as hilling up, so all Québec growers are forced to bury their vines before the snow falls.

DID YOU KNOW?

Hilling up adds an extra 7 to 10 percent to the cost of a bottle of wine.

SAQ Control

In Québec, all alcohol sales are regulated by the Société des alcools du Québec (SAQ). Most alcoholic beverages are sold through SAQ stores throughout the province, although wine, beer and other low-alcohol beverages can be sold in grocery stores and dépanneurs (convenience stores)—Québec is the only province in Canada to allow this. Grocers purchase their alcohol products through SAQ wholesale outlets.

The SAQ dates back to 1921, when the provincial government created the Commission des liqueurs de Québec as a response to the temperance movements and Prohibition (the Commission split into two separate bodies, the Société des alcools du Québec and the Commission de contrôle des permis d'alcool, in 1971). Québec only implemented Prohibition for a few weeks in 1919 before it was repealed, but temperance movements were still putting pressure on the provincial government to control the consumption of alcohol. The province created the Commission to control all aspects of the wine and alcohol industry, including imports, exports, sales and quality control. It was North America's first state liquor retailing monopoly.

DID YOU  KNOW?

During the 1920s and '30s in Québec, an individual could purchase only one bottle of spirits at a time. Wine, however, was not rationed.

ATLANTIC WINES

The Cradle of Canadian Wine

Nova Scotia, which lies midway between the equator and the North Pole, is a seemingly unlikely place to grow grapes. Yet the grape is no stranger to this province; wild vines were already growing in abundance here when settlers first arrived from Europe. The settlers made wine from these grapes almost immediately.

Nova Scotia is now home to nine wineries, six making wine from grapes and three making only fruit wines. Most of the wineries are located in the Annapolis Valley and surrounding areas and in the Gaspereau and Avon River valleys. Although another half dozen wineries are scattered throughout New Brunswick, Newfoundland and Prince Edward Island, none of these provinces boasts a wine industry that can rival Nova Scotia's in quality and quantity.

Fruitful Endeavour

The first commercial winery in the Atlantic region was Chipman Wines, which opened in 1941 near Kentville, Nova Scotia. The winery's first product was a hard apple cider called Golden Glow; the winery also produced wines from cherries, elderberries, blueberries and cranberries. Chipman began producing grape wines by bottling imported bulk wine in the early 1980s but closed in 1983, when it was purchased by Ontario-based Andrés Wines. Andrés had opened a bottling plant in 1965 in Truro, Nova Scotia, and acquired Chipman to eliminate the local competition. However, Andrés continued to bottle only imported grape wines; no wine grapes were grown on a commercial scale in Nova Scotia or the other Atlantic provinces until the late 1970s.

He's a Believer

Nova Scotia's first commercial grape winery opened its doors in 1980. Grand Pré Wines was a venture started by Roger Dial, an American who had studied winemaking in California and planted experimental grapevines in the Annapolis Valley in 1977. The vineyard consisted primarily of hybrid varieties, including two obscure Russian varieties, Michurinetz and Severnyi. Dial was a true believer in the grape, investing in all manner of businesses in the wine industry and resolutely championing Nova Scotia's potential as a winemaking province. Although Grand Pré was forced to close in 1987 because of financial difficulties, the winery reopened as Domaine de Grand Pré, after undergoing extensive renovations under its new owner, Swiss banker Hanspeter Stutz. Stutz replanted the vineyards and constructed a showcase winery and cellar. The new winery opened in 2000, becoming an immediate tourist destination. The wines are primarily made from hybrid varieties, though an experimental block of other varieties is being tested.

Hybrids Rule

The varieties that do well in Nova Scotia's cool climate are primarily hybrids. Some winemakers have experimented with cool-climate *vinifera* varieties, such as Chardonnay and Pinot Noir, but these plantings have yet to grow successfully. The most common white-grape varieties in Nova Scotia are L'Acadie Blanc, Seyval Blanc and New York Muscat; Maréchal Foch reigns supreme as Nova Scotia's most successful red. Although these wines are all characteristically high in acidity (like all wines from very cool climates), they partner well with the region's local seafood dishes.

Going Solo

Prince Edward Island has the fewest number of commercial wineries of all Canada's established wine regions—in fact, it has only one: Rossignol Estate Winery. John Rossignol planted a vineyard in 1993 on a hill overlooking Northumberland Strait and established a winery a year later. Rossignol initially grew a few *vinifera* varieties, such as Cabernet Franc, Pinot Noir and Chardonnay, in abandoned greenhouses leftover from PEI's failed tobacco industry. However, because of the extreme temperature fluctuations, even protected under glass during the winter, the vines only lasted for seven years. The winery still makes a few wines from Maréchal Foch, Seyval Blanc, Chardonnay and Pinot Cabernet Franc, as well as several fruit wines and mead. Rossignol is also experimenting with growing Pinot Noir vines in various pockets across the country.

Fruit Passion

New Brunswick's wine industry wasn't established until 1998, when the province's Department of Agriculture established a program with the fruit growers to allow the production of wine and distilled spirits. New Brunswick's first winery, Gagetown Cider Company, was established a year later to make apple cider and other fruit wines. A few other wineries followed suit over the next decade, including Belliveau Orchards and Waterside Farms. Winegarden Estate Winery & Distillery was the first winery in the province to make grape wines; it has since been followed by La Ferme Maury and Gillis of Belleisle Winery, which produce grape and fruit wines.

Working Together

Winegarden Estate Winery has led New Brunswick's wine industry by working collaboratively with many of the province's neophyte wineries. The company, founded in 1991 by Werner and Roswitha Rosswog, was the first private fruit distillery in the Atlantic provinces. In 1997, the company received a farm winery licence and began making wine and liqueurs. Winegarden has also provided the winemaking facilities for other New Brunswick wineries, including Ferme Maury, Tierney Point Winery and Tuddenham Farms. The winery also worked with Gagetown cider to make the province's first apple wines.

ONTARIO

The Lake Effect

Ontario's wine regions are located in the southern part of the province, along the coasts of the Great Lakes. The lakes provide a cooling effect in summer and a warming effect in the winter and work like enormous hot-water bottles, releasing heat slowly over time. Grapes grow in favoured little pockets that are protected from frost but open to the sun.

Niagara Peninsula

The Niagara Peninsula is home to a boggling array of fruits and vegetables; almost anything can grow in its fertile soil. More than 60 wineries are clustered in a few main areas of the Peninsula. Although Niagara is only an hour's drive from Toronto, it has little of the big-city feel, featuring instead stretches of lush green vineyards, interrupted by picturesque towns and pockets of suburbia.

What allows grapes to grow here is the Niagara Escarpment, a rocky bench of land rising from the shores of Lake Ontario. Warm air from the lake blows up the Escarpment and then tumbles back down in a circular motion, carrying away frost and preventing rot by drying the vines. The Escarpment was once the coastline of ancient Lake Iroquois and is some 430 million years old.

DID YOU KNOW?

You can taste the age of the land in Niagara's wines. The vines are grown on land rich with minerals deposited hundreds of millions of years ago by retreating glaciers. These minerals nourish the vines and give the wines complexity.

Winery Profile — Château des Charmes

Situated in a huge stone mansion in the middle of extensive vineyards, Château des Charmes is perhaps as close to a French-style winery as you'll find in Canada. The winery is owned by the Bosc family, which immigrated from France in the 1960s. Paul Michel Bosc, a fifth-generation winemaker and a major figure in Canada's wine industry, was the winemaker at Ontario's Château-Gai winery for 15 years before founding Château des Charmes in 1978. With his wife, Andrée, and sons, Pierre-Jean and Paul-André, Bosc has crafted an award-winning portfolio of French-style wines. Château des Charmes has also proven itself a valuable partner in wine research, investing in trials of grapevine clones best suited to Niagara's climate and testing new grape-growing and winemaking processes. To honour his service to the industry, Paul Bosc was invested with the Order of Canada in 2005.

DID YOU  KNOW?

Ontario's wine regions are located along the same latitude as the Chianti Classico region in Italy and the Rioja region in Spain.

Prince Edward County

Some believe it's folly to grow grapes in Prince Edward County; the weather is much cooler than Niagara, and if the vines aren't killed outright from the severe winters, the grapes often have trouble achieving full ripeness in the summer. But some winemakers have compared Prince Edward County to France's Burgundy region, because of its cool climate and limestone-rich soil. Investments have been pouring into the area, some of them quite grand, which is almost unheard of for a region that still hasn't really proven itself. Only time will tell if those Chardonnay and Pinot Noir vines will produce a product similar to European wines. One thing is certain— producing high-quality wines won't be easy, especially given the region's brutally cold winters. Temperatures regularly drop to –30°C, cold enough to kill *Vitis vinifera* grapevines. Intensive winter management techniques are required, including covering the vines with earth in the fall.

Although its wine merits are still in the trial phase—the county's first wineries were established in 1999 and 2000, and vines have been growing here only since the mid-1990s—there's no denying the attraction of the landscape. An island located just off the north shore of Lake Ontario, midway between Toronto and Kingston, Prince Edward County boasts more than 800 kilometres of shoreline. Its rolling pastures and quaint villages offer relief from the hectic pace of city life. The county has created a strong agri-tourism infrastructure, which includes a well-established winery route, taste trail and annual wine events and tastings—despite the fact that the region has fewer than a dozen wineries!

DID YOU KNOW?

Prince Edward County was settled by United Empire Loyalists, who fled the American Revolution in the early 1800s.

Huff Estates Winery

Although it has been open for less than a decade, Huff Estates Winery has already firmly established its reputation as Prince Edward County's must-see winery. It was founded by Frank Huff, a descendant of United Empire Loyalists and a former chemical engineer, who made his fortune in the plastics business before turning to wine. The winery, a state-of-the-art, gravity-fed operation, overlooks several acres of vineyards from its position on Mount Pleasant, one of the highest points in the county. Its elevated position allows Huff Estates' winemaking processes to be powered largely by gravity, with the liquid flowing down to the sunken cellar. The winery even boasts a helicopter pad, designed to aid corporate getaways to the nearby country inn.

Lake Erie North Shore

Although Lake Erie North Shore is a small wine region, it is one of Canada's foremost up-and-coming regions, with wineries opening at a rapid rate. It is also Ontario's most historic wine region. The area, also known as Essex County, was the epicentre of Ontario wine production in the late 1800s. Dozens of wineries were in operation at the time, and, though the region has since been surpassed by Niagara (in production quantity), producers here are rooted in a solid wine tradition.

The Lake Erie North Shore region is located along Canada's only southern coast—the north shore of Lake Erie. It is warmer than Niagara, owing to its more southerly location and greater exposure to large bodies of water. The region boasts 12 wineries, though more are slated to open in late 2009 and 2010.

DID YOU KNOW?

Wine isn't Lake Erie North Shore's only attraction—scuba divers flock to Pelee Passage, a treacherous, reef-ridden strip with more than 200 shipwrecks stretching along 35 kilometres.

Winery Profile — Colio Estate Wines

Founded in 1980, Colio is the oldest operating winery in Lake Erie North Shore. It is also a commercial winery, housing more than 1.2 million litres of wine in its enormous barrel cellar. Despite its high production volume, Colio has maintained consistently good quality across its extensive wine portfolio. The winery was founded by Enzo de Luca, an Italian expatriate who grew up drinking wines from the northeastern Italian region of Collio— hence the winery's name.

Pelee Island

Pelee Island, located roughly 25 kilometres off the mainland of southern Ontario in Lake Erie, is Canada's smallest wine region and also its oldest—the ivy-covered stone ruins of Canada's first commercial winery, Vin Villa, can still be seen here. The island enjoys a mild climate, thanks to the moderating effect of the surrounding lake. It is also home to a huge diversity of wildlife, with more than 10,000 native species of plants and animals. The island is on the migration path for numerous species of birds as well as the monarch butterfly. In addition to the plentiful waterfowl, other common sights are red foxes, rabbits, wild turkeys and even flying squirrels. Many of these creatures adorn the labels of the island's only winery.

DID YOU KNOW?

The Niagara Peninsula, Pelee Island and Lake Erie North Shore regions supply 80 percent of the Canadian-grown grapes used in Canadian wine production.

Winery Profile — **Pelee Island Winery**

Although it shares its name with the island, Pelee Island Winery is actually located on the mainland, at Kingsville. The grapes are ferried across from the island during harvest—so if you happen to visit in autumn, be prepared to share the ferry with a load of grapes. The winery was founded in 1984 by Wolf von Teichman and the Strehn family, natives of Austria. This heritage is reflected in the wines made here, especially the Zweigelt, a native Austrian grape variety. However, though the mainland winery is the site of the actual winemaking, it's the Pelee Island Wine Pavilion that draws the biggest crowd. The pavilion is situated in a large, contemporary barn building and features an outdoor patio, a museum of winemaking equipment and numerous other historical wine artifacts.

Toronto and Surrounding Area

Although they don't have the aesthetic benefit of surrounding fields of vineyards, urban wineries offer a quick and convenient way for visitors to sample wines that aren't readily available elsewhere. The Greater Toronto Area has several wineries within its limits. Grapes for their wines are usually purchased and trucked in from nearby growers, although a few wineries do have their own vineyard sites.

Winery Profile — Magnotta Winery Corporation

The Magnotta Winery Corporation is a staple of Ontario's wine scene—and a sight to behold. The company was founded in 1990 by Gabe and Rossana Magnotta and boasts the third-largest sales volume in Ontario. The facility is enormous: the 55,700 square-metre building houses not just the winery but a distillery and brewery as well. Magnotta owns more than 73 hectares of vineyards throughout Niagara, as well as a 142-hectare vineyard in Chile that supplies juice and wine. The winery's extensive portfolio includes such unique creations as the world's first icewine grappa, the first eau-de-vie distilled from icewine and an Amarone-inspired red wine.

DID YOU KNOW?

Ontario has more than 6500 hectares of vineyards, almost double British Columbia's vineyard area.

QUÉBEC

A River Runs Through It

Although Québec has not adopted the VQA system—the industry is simply too small to merit this—it does have five clearly defined wine regions, which are located in the southern part of the province along the St. Lawrence River, beginning just west of Montréal and continuing northeast to Québec City.

DID YOU  KNOW?

Because the majority of Québec's wines are blends of different grapes, sometimes from different years, they are usually labelled under proprietary names.

 **Domaine des Côtes d'Ardoise**

Domaine des Côtes d'Ardoise is the winery that spearheaded winemaking in the Cantons-de-l'Est region. Founder Christian Barthomeuf established a vineyard just west of Dunham in 1979 and opened his winery a year later. The area experiences a unique microclimate that protects it from frost and allows the growth of a few *Vitis vinifera* varieties, such as Riesling and Gamay. Rising around the winery in a horseshoe shape and protected by woods on all sides, the vineyard is dotted with numerous sculptures made by Canadian artists; a monarch butterfly made from an old railway snowplow stands at the highest point. When Barthomeuf retired in 1984, he passed the winery into the capable hands of Jacques Papillon. Domaine des Côtes d'Ardoise has a portfolio of 11 wines.

Cantons-de-l'Est

French for "Eastern Townships," Cantons-de-l'Est was named by settlers who came to the area in the 18th century. It is the cradle of Québécois viticulture and the site of the province's first modern vineyards. Wine lovers from all over the world flock to the area's two dozen wineries, especially during the annual "Fête des Vendanges"—a harvest festival in September, held in the town of Magog.

Montérégie

The Montérégie region is Québec's bread basket—or apple basket, as it were. The region is home to numerous crops, and the town of Rougemont is the apple capital of Québec—in spring, the landscape is snow white from all the apple blossoms. Competing for the wine tourists' dollars are chocolate sellers, fruit growers, cider makers and market gardeners.

Winery Profile — Vignoble Angell

As luck would have it, the area around Vignoble Angell has one of the longest growing seasons in Québec—it is longer than the province's average season by two weeks. This extended warmth allows owner Jean-Guy Angell to grow some of Québec's very few plantings of *Vitis vinifera*, with which he makes a tiny amount of Chardonnay, Merlot and Pinot Noir. The operation is also one of the province's earlier ventures; it was established in 1978, when Jean-Guy planted 200 vines. The winery opened its doors in 1985. The wines are currently made by his son, Guy.

Lanaudière

One of the first areas of New France to be settled and one of the first agricultural regions in Québec, Lanaudière provided early settlers with everything from tobacco to maple syrup. It is a relatively new grape-growing region; only three wineries are located within the area, which stretches along the north shore of the St. Lawrence.

 **Domaine de l'Île Ronde**

Without a doubt, this newly renovated winery steals the attention in Lanaudière. Located on an island in the St. Lawrence River, Domaine de l'Île Ronde is extravagant. Perhaps befitting its location, the winery's architecture is a hybrid of traditional French châteaux and contemporary American. The owner, Jocelyn Lafortune, keeps the nine-hectare vineyard—the most densely planted in the province—in immaculate condition. Domaine de l'Île Ronde specializes in fortified wines; although Lafortune currently buys the spirits necessary for making these wines, he hopes one day to have his own still.

Québec City

Although a forbidding place of stiff winds and arctic temperatures for a good chunk of the year, Québec City is home to a handful of wineries, notably Vignobles du Faubourg, Isle de Bacchus, and Sainte-Pétronille, most of which produce wines made from hybrid varieties. Domaine Royarnois even makes a few wines from the *riparia* grape species and is one of the few wineries left in Canada to work with these grapes.

Vignobles Bourg Royal, le Nordet and la Source à Marguerite produce cider and iced cider, and le Moulin du Petit Pré makes an excellent raspberry liqueur.

The modern wine industry began late in this area; wine grapes just wouldn't survive until better winter-protection techniques were employed. Regardless of the improvements, Québec City's vines must be grown within sight of the mighty St. Lawrence River—the water reflects sunlight back onto the vines and helps them ripen. The river also helps regulate the temperature in the winter. Although the region's wine trade is still in its fledgling stage, it has great support from the booming tourism industry.

DID YOU  KNOW?

The first modern vineyard in the Québec City region was an experimental plot planted at Beauport in 1979.

Winery Profile **Vignoble le Moulin du Petit Pré**

One of Québec's main tourist attractions, Vignoble le Moulin du Petit Pré is located in the basement of a historic flour mill built in 1695; the water-driven mill is still used to make stone-ground organic flour. Established in 1995, the winery makes grape wines from its four hectares of vines, as well as fruit wines made from currants, raspberries and Saskatoon berries. Petit Pré also hosts an annual harvest festival, Fête de Vendanges, in the fall.

Basses-Laurentides

Basses-Laurentides is a tiny region, home to only a handful of wineries—which makes visiting them all quick and easy. It is the westernmost wine region in Québec, hugging the northern shore of the St. Lawrence River.

DID YOU  KNOW?

The largest apiary in Québec, Intermiel, resides within the town of St-Benoît de Mirabel. The company makes an interesting honey wine (also known as mead) and produces honey, beeswax, royal jelly and many other bee products.

La Roche des Brises

La Roche des Brises was founded in 1993 by Jean-Pierre Bélisle and was the first winery on Montréal's north shore. Easily the region's biggest tourist destination, it is home to a five-star country inn, one of the best restaurants in the province, tens of thousands of grapevines and more than 1000 apple trees. Bélisle is active in the province's wine industry as president of Les Vignerons du Québec, working to push the provincial government for more support of the local wine industry. The winery specializes in late-harvest wines made from hybrid varieties, which are similar in style to the Vendange Tardive wines made in France's Alsace region.

NOVA SCOTIA

Valley Vintners

Nova Scotia has not adopted the VQA system, because its wine industry is too small. However, the province does boast six wine regions, which are scattered throughout the province. Although most of these regions are home to only one or two wineries, these numbers are expected to swell in the coming years.

Annapolis Valley

The Annapolis Valley is the heart of Nova Scotia's wine industry and has been farmed for centuries. The warmest area in the province, the valley is ideal for wine production. It runs along Nova Scotia's western coast, from Wolfville in the northeast to Annapolis Royal in the southwest.

DID YOU KNOW?

The Annapolis Valley has been dubbed Canada's "first breadbasket."

Blomidon Estate Winery

Blomidon Estate Winery is owned by Peter Jensen and Laura McCain, proprietors of Ontario's Creekside Estate and Paragon Vineyards, who purchased the property in 1997. The vineyards are situated on a hill sloping down to the Bay of Fundy, and the winery features a dazzling view of ☞

Winery Profile

the bay. The original vineyard was planted in 1986, and its first grapes were sold to Roger Dial at Domaine de Grand Pré. In 2003, Blomidon gained the distinction of marketing Nova Scotia's first Chardonnay since the 1984 and 1985 bottlings released by Grand Pré, and in 2009, the wine earned a medal at the All Canadian Wine Championships. Blomidon's success with this grape could herald a new phase in the Nova Scotia wine industry; other wineries have already begun experimenting with Chardonnay and other *vinifera* varieties.

Gaspereau Valley and Avon River Valley

The Gaspereau and Avon River valleys, located east of Annapolis Valley, are being developed as wine-growing areas. There are only two wineries in each region. Vines were not planted in Gaspereau until the mid-1990s, and the first commercial winery in the area wasn't established until 2003. The Avon River Valley has a slightly longer viticultural history; its Saint-Famille winery was established in 1989.

DID YOU KNOW?

Much of the agricultural land in the Avon River Valley was reclaimed from the salt marshes by the Acadians. They constructed dykes in the latter half of the 1600s to drain the rich soil from the mud flats.

Sainte-Famille Wines

The Sainte-Famille winery, in the Avon River Valley, is located on the site of an old Acadian village known as La Paroisse Sainte-Famille de Pisiquit, which was settled in 1685. The winery is named for the local parish and was founded by Suzanne and Doug Corkum in 1989. The Corkums had entered the wine industry a decade earlier as grape growers, supplying Roger Dial's nearby Domaine de Grand Pré winery. However, when Grand Pré closed, and the Corkums lost their only market, they began making their own wine. The winery now produces more than 6000 cases annually, from hybrids and a few *vinifera* varieties.

Malagash Peninsula

The Malagash might be isolated, but it has an agreeable climate and a well-established tourism industry. It is also home to the province's largest winery, Jost. This has successfully put Malagash on the Nova Scotia wine map, despite its relative obscurity. The coming years will no doubt see further development of the wine industry in this land of coastal inlets and gentle hills.

Jost Vineyards

Jost Vineyards is the only winery to call the Malagash home. As Nova Scotia's biggest winery, producing more than 35,000 cases annually, Jost has carved a firm place for itself in this remote region. Despite its size, Jost is a family affair; ☞

Winery
Profile

it was founded in 1978, when Hans Wilhelm Jost planted a vineyard. The winery was established a few years later, in 1983. Jost's son, Hans Christian, now makes all the wines in Jost's extensive portfolio of almost 40 offerings.

LaHave River Valley

LaHave has one of the mildest climates in Nova Scotia, which allows it to grow numerous grapes—even a few cool-weather *vinifera* varieties, such as Chardonnay and Pinot Noir. The soil is also the same as that found in the Annapolis Valley on the other side of the province, thanks to glacial activity during the Quaternary Period, which extended from 75,000 to 10,000 years ago. As the glaciers moved over the land, they picked up and carried along soil, rocks and other minerals; when the glaciers melted, these soils and minerals (in the case of Nova Scotia, that distinct red earth) were left behind in different areas. This red earth combines with LaHave's deep layers of sand, gravel and slate to give a distinct mineral element to the grapes grown here.

Winery Profile — Petite Rivière Vineyards

Although Petite Rivière Vineyards has only been around for a few years, the winery's roots are deep in LaHave's history. It was founded by Philip Wamboldt, whose ancestors have been in the area for 10 generations. Wamboldt first planted vines in 1994, starting with the Harmon's Hill Vineyard and expanding to a second, St. Mary's Vineyard, in 2000. The winery—the region's first commercial winery—followed a few years later, opening in 2004. The difference in soil between the two vineyard sites produces grapes with noticeable differences, and blending them produces wines with great depth and complexity.

DID YOU KNOW?

The symbol of Nova Scotia and one of Canada's prominent icons, the *Bluenose* schooner (whose image can be seen on the Canadian dime) is part of LaHave's rich history. Schooners such as this were widely used in the past as fishing boats by the area's first settlers.

BRITISH COLUMBIA

Islands and Valleys

British Columbia has two main growing regions: the desert-like Okanagan and Similkameen valleys and the coastal Fraser Valley and Vancouver Island. The sprawling 160-kilometre stretch of the Okanagan Valley is by far the largest region, with the majority of BC's wineries residing somewhere along the shores of Lake Okanagan.

DID YOU  KNOW?

Lake Okanagan is reputed to be the home of a lake monster named Ogopogo, described as a snake-like creature more than 4.5 metres long. Prospect Winery, a brand of entry-level wines from Mission Hill, named its Ogopogo's Lair Pinot Grigio for the local monster.

Okanagan Valley

Although the Okanagan Valley has a desert-like climate, because of its sheer size, it has numerous microclimates. In general, the summers are long, hot and dry, and the winters are very cold. Most of the region is so dry, in fact, that all vineyards must use irrigation. The area just north of the Okanagan is noticeably cooler and greener, thanks to higher annual rainfall, but because it is at the extreme northern latitude of grape cultivation, a limited number of varieties do well there, mainly whites and a few red hybrids. The southern region, around Oliver and Osoyoos, is a desert zone, with low scrub brushes and grasses. The blistering daytime heat ensures that innumerable varieties ripen fully, and the drop in temperatures overnight ensures that the grapes retain acidity.

DID YOU KNOW?

Mount Boucherie, a mountain near Kelowna, is an extinct volcano. The Mt. Boucherie Estate Winery takes its name from this landform.

Winery Profile **Red Rooster Winery**

Red Rooster is fast becoming one of the Okanagan Valley's mainstays. Founded in 1997 by Beat and Prudence Mahrer, a Swiss couple who emigrated to Canada in 1990, the winery quickly gained popularity for its award-winning wines. A new winemaking facility, finished in 2004, was built to accommodate this success. The eye-catching, cathedral-style building is a popular tourist destination. In addition to making great wines, Red Rooster has also established itself as a patron of the arts; the works of numerous local

☞

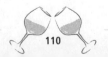

Winery Profile

artists can be seen throughout the facility, and the winery hosts an annual Bohemian Wine Festival for visual artists of all genres to show how they create their works.

A controversial piece of local art also resides within Red Rooster's walls. *The Baggage Handler,* also known as Frank, is a sculpture depicting a naked man carrying a suitcase. The sculpture, which now stands in Red Rooster's tasting room, was originally located in Penticton's Marina Way traffic circle. A huge uproar followed the statue's unveiling (pardon the pun), resulting in a band of locals knocking the statue off its pedestal and dismembering it. In honour of the sculpture (and perhaps in an attempt to restore its dignity), Red Rooster released a wine in its name: Cabernet Frank 2004, featuring a photo of the statue on the label.

DID YOU  KNOW?

Canada's only true desert is located at the southern end of the Okanagan, around the town of Osoyoos. Although the desert is only about 24 kilometres long, it is considered the northernmost extension of the Great Basin Desert, which extends south through the United States and into the Sonoran Desert in Mexico.

Similkameen Valley
The Similkameen Valley is one of Canada's smallest wine regions; five wineries call it home. The valley is hot and arid, much like the southern Okanagan, and is ideal for growing

fruit of all kinds. Like the Okanagan, the entire area must be irrigated; the blistering heat and blustery winds rob the soil of its moisture in seconds.

DID YOU KNOW?

The community of Keremeos, the hub of the Similkameen Valley, is known as the "Fruit Stand Capital of Canada."

Winery Profile — St. Laszlo Vineyards Estate Winery

St. Laszlo was the first winery built in the Similkameen Valley. It was named for the Yugoslavian town of St. Laszlo, where founder Joe Ritlop was born. True to his roots, Ritlop's wines are all made in a traditional, Eastern European style. He also deserves credit for planting an eclectic mix of grapes; the winery grows everything from standard European varieties to rare American hybrids such as Clinton and Interlaken—St. Laszlo is almost certainly the only winery in Canada making varietal wines from these grapes. The winery also makes numerous fruit wines, including an intriguing concoction made from rose petals.

St. Laszlo was the first Canadian winery to commercially sell icewine. Like Walter Hainle, Ritlop saw an opportunity to make icewine when an early winter froze unpicked grapes in 1984. He entered the wine in a BC competition the following year—but, because there was no icewine category at the time, the wine was refused.

Vancouver Island and the Wine Islands

Bet you never thought Canada was home to a place called "the Wine Islands." But it's true; half a dozen wineries are scattered throughout the four small Gulf Islands between Vancouver Island and the mainland, and Vancouver Island itself boasts 22 wineries. Most of Vancouver Island's vineyards are located on the Saanich Peninsula north of Victoria and the Cowichan Valley, around Duncan. Because the region is still very young, many wineries supplement locally grown grapes with those sourced from other areas of BC, mainly the Okanagan.

The Duncan Project

The first commercial vineyard on Vancouver Island was established in 1970 by Dennis Zanatta, on a former dairy farm in the Cowichan Valley, just south of the town of Duncan. Zanatta was an Italian immigrant with a love for the grape, and his experiments with various grape varieties did not go unnoticed. The provincial government, quickly picking up on the potential of vineyards in this area, used Zanatta's vineyard to assess more than 100 different grape varieties. The test became known as the Duncan Project, which ran from 1983 to 1990. Unfortunately, the project ran out of funding before a truly accurate report could be made of the grape trials. Ortega, Pinot Gris and Auxerrois were identified as prime varieties for the region, but, according to the final report, 20 to 30 more years of testing were needed to gain reliable conclusions. The report hasn't daunted several winemakers, who have conducted their own tests of the island's viticultural potential. The Cowichan Valley is still regarded as the prime grape-growing area, though other isolated pockets of prime grape land on Vancouver Island might yet be revealed.

Blue Grouse Estate Winery

Blue Grouse winery is the realization of a BC wine pioneer's dream: the vineyards are located on the site of Vancouver Island's first vineyard, which was planted by John Harper. Harper worked in the BC wine industry for decades, as a vineyard worker for both Andrés and Jordan Ste. Michelle in the 1970s. He advised many island growers about which vines to cultivate but never made wine on a commercial scale.

In 1988, Hans and Evangeline Klitz emigrated to Canada from Germany and bought a farm on Vancouver Island. They found a neglected vineyard on the property—Harper's own plot. The wine bug kicked in quickly; Hans revived the vineyard and began making wine as a hobby. That hobby turned into a serious pursuit in 1993, with the establishment of a commercial winery. Blue Grouse's wines are clean and pure, a style reflective of Hans' extensive background in science; he ensures that all the chemical constituents of the wine are in proper proportions. A former veterinarian, Hans has degrees in veterinary medicine, tropical veterinary medicine and fish pathology and also has a doctorate in microbiology!

DID YOU KNOW?

Blue Grouse takes its name from the birds that live in the area and are regular visitors to the vineyard.

Fraser Valley

Although the Fraser Valley region accounts for only slightly more than one percent of BC's vineyard acreage, it is quickly establishing itself as the next up-and-coming area. The climate is tempered by the Pacific Ocean, and the mild coastal winters seldom present danger of damage from freezing. Most of the grapes grown here are white varieties; because reds often don't ripen fully in the coastal climate, the region's red wines are usually made from grapes brought in from the Okanagan. The biggest viticultural threat is the humidity, which promotes fungus, mould and mildew. However, coping with humidity is one of the easier challenges of Canadian winemaking; with careful pruning techniques to allow air circulation and judicious spraying for rot, growers can successfully dodge most serious problems.

Half a dozen wineries call the Fraser Valley home; most of them are clustered near the U.S. border. A bonus of this region is that Vancouver is only a short drive away—its proximity will certainly help promote the area as a wine destination in the coming years.

Winery Profile **Domaine de Chaberton Estate Winery**

Domaine de Chaberton is the trail blazer of BC's coastal wineries. The Fraser Valley's first significant commercial vineyard was established in 1981 by Claude and Ingeborg Violet, who planted 16 hectares of white varieties, including Ortega, Bacchus, Madeleine Angevine and Madeleine Sylvaner. A decade later, in 1991, the Violets opened the Domaine de Chaberton winery. The vineyards grow only white varieties; red grapes are sourced from vineyards in

Winery
Profile

the Okanagan's Black Sage Road. The Violets retired in 2005, passing on the torch to Anthony Cheng and Eugene Kwan.

WEIRD WINE NAMES

Uncle Ben's Gourmet Wines

No, these wines aren't made by a rice manufacturer. In 1969, Ben Ginter bought British Columbia's Mission Hill winery. After struggling financially for years, Mission Hill was on the verge of bankruptcy by the end of the 1960s and was forced to sell. Ginter, who had made his fortune in the construction business and clearly did not suffer a lack of ego, immediately changed the name of the winery to Uncle Ben's Gourmet Winery. In addition to renaming the winery for himself, he also put his portrait on the wine labels.

Fuddle Duck

Fuddle Duck, one of Uncle Ben's Gourmet Wines, belonged to the menagerie of pop wines that rose to great popularity in the 1970s. Pop wines were modelled on the hugely successful example set by Baby Duck and often bore similar names. Fuddle Duck, however, is unique because its name was derived from former Canadian Prime Minister Pierre Trudeau's infamous "fuddle duddle" comment.

In 1971, opposition members alleged that Trudeau mouthed an obscenity in the House of Commons. When confronted, Trudeau denied uttering an expletive, though he did admit to moving his lips. When pressed to state what he was mouthing, he responded sarcastically by asking the rhetorical question: "What is the nature of your thoughts, gentlemen, when you say 'fuddle duddle' or something like that?"

Through the telephone-game effect of the media (and perhaps because it rhymes with the alleged obscenity), Trudeau's comment became known as "fuddle duck." Many sources reported that Trudeau admitted to having said "fuddle duck," instead of the alleged expletive. Parliamentary scandals aside, the words certainly make a colourful wine label.

Laughing Stock Vineyards

Laughing Stock Vineyards is owned and operated by the husband-and-wife team of David and Cynthia Enns. A former investment manager, David traded a career in the stock market for one in the vineyard but used his previous career as inspiration for the name and branding of his current venture. The names of the winery and wines are obvious references to his former profession—and each bottle is printed with stock market ticker tape, featuring the closing prices of selected stocks from the day the grapes were picked. The NASDAQ twines around the Chardonnay, while the S&P 500 wraps around the Portfolio. Starting up a winery is a risky venture, but the Enns proved that if it's done right, you can laugh all the way to the bank.

Portfolio Red

Although the name may seem frivolous, the wines are anything but—Laughing Stock's Portfolio red, its flagship Bordeaux blend, was branded with cult-wine status early in the winery's history. This tiny operation—just a few acres of vineyard tucked away on the Naramata Bench in the Okanagan—launched itself onto the Canadian wine scene in 2003, with the release of its first vintage. All 800 cases, 500 of the Portfolio red and 300 of the Chardonnay, sold out within two weeks— immediately establishing Laughing Stock as BC's newest cult winery.

DID YOU  KNOW?

Just after it was released, Laughing Stock's Portfolio won a gold medal at the 2007 Canadian Wine Awards.

Wildass

Wildass is one of the first examples of a "declassified" Canadian wine. Common in Europe, especially among the famous wineries in such hallowed regions as Bordeaux and Tuscany, declassified wines are wines that a producer bottles under a second label, because the wine either doesn't meet quality standards for the first label or doesn't meet the appellation's laws. These declassified second labels often represent killer values, because, although the wine is often almost as good as the winery's first offering, it's sold at a fraction of the price.

Wildass wine is made by Stratus, one of Canada's premium wine producers. Initially only available at local restaurants in Niagara, Wildass achieved such popularity that a limited number of bottles are now sold online and at liquor stores across the country. Although Stratus' main offerings are serious wines, meant to be served with food or cellared for several years, Wildass was only ever meant to be a fun, bistro-style wine that you could quaff at any time. But the suggestive name makes it a no-brainer gift for carefree and mulish wine drinkers alike.

Blasted Church

The labels on this Okanagan wine tell the story of its namesake. Blasted Church is named for a wooden church originally located in a mining encampment in Fairview, BC. The church was dismantled and moved 26 kilometres away in 1929 to a site near Okanagan Falls. Four sticks of dynamite, lit by the parish priest, were used to loosen the wooden nails holding the rafters together—but the blast also succeeded in toppling the steeple. Blasted Church's labels depict the destruction of the church and witty caricatures of wine writers and critics, including Robert Parker and *Wine Spectator* publisher Marvin Shanken. The labels, created by Vancouver designer Bernie Hadley-Beauregard and executed by Toronto illustrator Monika Melnychuk, are fast becoming collector's items.

DID YOU  KNOW?

In 2004, Blasted Church was the first winery in the Okanagan to bottle most of its wines with screw-cap closures.

Dynamite Wines

Blasted Church was founded by Chris and Evelyn Campbell, former accountants who retired from the world of numbers in 2002 and moved to the Okanagan to make wine. The pair purchased a winery that had been established in 1998 by Croatian grape grower Dan Prpich and changed the name from the difficult-to-pronounce Prpich Hills to its current fiery moniker. Unfortunately, the winery has had rather bad luck with winemakers. Its first, Frank Supernak, a veteran Okanagan winemaker, died suddenly in an accident just after the winery opened. The Campbells then hired Willem Grobbelaar, who made the 2003 vintage. However, Grobbelaar was forced to return to his home country of South Africa when his Canadian visa was not renewed the following year. For the 2004 vintage, the winery hired Marcus Ansems, an Australian who previously worked at Ontario's Creekside winery. The current winemaker is Richard Kanazawa, an Australian and former professional rugby player.

(Ir)Reverent Wines

Building on the connotations of the winery name, Blasted Church has named its wines in similarly quirky fashion. Its top tier of wines, which includes a Chardonnay, Cabernet Sauvignon and Malbec-Syrah blend, belong to the "Revered" series. Other wittily named wines include Amen Port-de-Merlot, The Dam Flood, Mixed Blessings and Hatfield's Fuse, which is named for the parish priest who detonated the dynamite that blasted the church apart.

Megalomaniac

As the wine labels and website will tell you, Megalomaniac owner John Howard initially planned to name his winery for himself. However, his friends accused him of being just another "[profanity withheld] megalomaniac"—and the name stuck. Although Howard might make this out to be a regrettable occurrence, the name has certainly inspired a plethora of witty names and label designs.

Howard began the winery as a retirement project in 2007. No stranger to the Canadian wine industry, Howard had already proven his mettle as owner of Vineland Estates, raising the winery's profile to its current status as one of Niagara's best Riesling producers. Although he might be a serious player in the wine business, Howard doesn't take himself seriously— and this is evidenced by the names he has chosen for the Megalomaniac series. Narcissist Riesling, My Way Chardonnay, Bigmouth Merlot, Pink Slip Pinot Noir Rose and SonOfaBitch Pinot Noir (so named because Pinot is an SOB to make) are just a few examples of Howard's quirky sense of humour.

Vainglorious Cabernet Merlot
The wines' labelling completes the picture of Megalomaniac's quirky marketing. Consider the description for the winery's Vainglorious Cabernet-Merlot: "Far from humble, this Cabernet Merlot swells with pride, and basks in its own self-importance. Although we are loathe to admit it, its behaviour is completely justified."

Long Dog Vineyard & Winery

The name of this winery is more literal than idiosyncratic—Long Dog is named for the dachshunds that occupy an honoured spot in the operation. Although owners James Lahti and Victoria Rose initially intended the 1840s farmhouse and surrounding 121 hectares to house themselves and their film-editing business, their love of wine lured them into experimenting with growing grapes—as many of their neighbours were already doing. With the help of close friend Steven Rapkin, test batches of vines were planted in spring 2000, and a latent viticultural drive was unleashed. Within a few years, Long Dog had become a full winery operation, producing Burgundy-style Chardonnay and Pinot Noir.

Elongated Canines

Given the partners' close connection to the dachshund breed, the name of Long Dog winery is only natural. Co-owner Victoria Rose grew up with dachshunds, and, when her husband and winery partner, James Lahti, gave her a dachshund puppy named Otto for her 30th birthday, he soon found himself devoted to the breed as well. The couple's friend and winery partner, Steven Rapkin, also took a liking to the elongated canines.

Unfortunately, Otto died suddenly of heart failure in 1998. His ashes are buried under a Pinot Noir vine planting—in essence, his memory lives on in the wines. Long Dog's current long dogs are Bella and Fanny.

UNUSUAL DIVERSIONS

Patio Vineyards

Not all Canadian vintners think big. Some think small—even tiny. Take the Africus Rex vineyard near Toronto, for example, which is quite possibly the world's only micro-winery. Africus Rex, a so-called patio vineyard, is believed to be the smallest in the world, at 2.1 metres long by 3.4 metres square. Owner Jeff Chorniak is a bonsai enthusiast, and his vineyard is composed of 26 Cabernet Franc bonsai vines. The bonsai vines stand 30 to 35 centimetres high and are grown hydroponically.

Tiny Wines

Although short in stature, the miniature vines at Africus Rex vineyard do yield small clusters of grapes; although smaller than bunches from a regular-sized vine, they're not miniature. Chorniak uses these grapes to make wine in his cellar. The entire winery, including the cellar, totals 10 square metres. He also sells the vines, so if you'd like to take a shot at making your own miniature wines, Africus Rex sells bonsai vines for about US$100 each. You get your pick of Chardonnay, Zinfandel, Cabernet Franc or Cabernet Sauvignon.

Straight Shooters

Vignoble la Bauge is one of Québec's stalwart wineries, courageously making wine in this region's unforgiving climate. Perhaps because making wine here can be such a frustrating pursuit, the Naud family developed a way to deal with the stress. The late Alcide Naud was a dairy farmer for several decades before he began making wine. At the same time that he developed his vineyard, he diversified his dairy farm and began raising an array of exotic animals. Naud also set up a protected terrain nearby for these animals, which he hunted with a crossbow.

At La Bauge, you can board a trolley that takes you through the vineyards. As it winds through the woods, you are likely to see a veritable menagerie of creatures, including such exotic species as South American reas, European deer, Australian emus, Japanese Sika deer and wild boar. Until 2002, visitors to the winery were allowed to bow-hunt wild boars. Although hunting is no longer allowed on the winery property, La Bauge owns a tract of land nearby on which hunting for wild boars is still permitted. For those less inclined to do the hunting themselves, the wine shop sells wild boar pâté, venison sausages and other exotic products.

DID YOU KNOW?

La Bauge means "wild boar" in French.

Aerial Adventures

Who would have thought that being an amateur pilot would have applications in the wine world? In perhaps the most bizarre—and desperate—attempt to drive off a flock of hungry birds, vineyard manager and amateur pilot John Barnay of Monashee Vineyards took to the skies to fight them on their own turf—or air, I suppose. Barnay flew an ultra-light aircraft back and forth over the vineyards for an entire afternoon, chasing a huge flock of birds in circles around the vineyard's airspace. As dramatic as this spectacle was (I'm sure no one got any work done that day), Barnay's victory was disappointingly short-lived. The birds were back within half an hour of the plane's landing.

Feathered Pest Control

Louise Engel of Featherstone Estate Winery has a better way to rid her vineyard of pesky birds. Engel, who obtained her licence in professional falconry in 2005, trained Amadeus, a male Harris's hawk, to scare off members of the resident bird population. Harris's hawks are native to South America, and they usually eat rabbits, but Engel has trained Amadeus to only hunt birds. He catches an average of one bird per day during the growing season—a small number, which doesn't have much direct effect on the local population, but it's enough to deter the birds from dwelling too long amid the vineyard's ripe fruit.

Equestrian Exploits

Paul Bosc, owner of Ontario's Château des Charmes winery, is a dedicated equestrian. He has his own horse-breeding stable and is absolutely passionate about his Egyptian Arabian horses. After tasting some of the winery's fabulous, French-style wines, visitors to the winery can go for a horseback ride. In fact, Château des Charmes is Canada's only combined horse farm and commercial vineyard.

Equine Wine

In homage to his passion for horses, Bosc named his flagship Bordeaux blend Equuleus. Equuleus, Latin for "little horse," is also the name of a constellation. In Greek mythology, Equuleus is the small half-brother of the much-more-famous Pegasus. The label of Château des Charmes' Equuleus features a stylized picture of one of the stable's horses—its most recent is a depiction of Eddie, a young stallion.

HOCKEY NIGHT IN WINE COUNTRY

Celebrity Wines

The celebrity wine movement is credited by many as a good thing, because it has given the Canadian wine industry plenty of exposure—what type of exposure, however, is up for debate. Although they've won both praise and damnation, celebrity wines are all too commonly not the greatest values. After all, the idea is to use big names to sell big volumes—the juice itself doesn't need to be that good.

On the upside, celebrity wines are often marketed to people who don't normally drink wine. Although they might not represent the best of our country's winemaking industry, if a wine with the Great One's name on it can get beer-lovin' NHL fans to start drinking wine, can you really condemn it?

Fans versus Foes

Opinions are split on the impact and significance of Canada's celebrity wines. Some argue that they provide a much-needed infusion of interest into the industry—many more people know about Gretzky than Grenache, and these wines provide a springboard for novices to develop an interest in wine. Others say that a celebrity's interest in wine is no more than investment diversification and that his or her goals are merely self-serving and money-oriented. Of course, this argument is offset by efforts from celebrities such as Wayne Gretzky and Mike Weir, whose net proceeds go to charity.

False Images

Motivations aside, one issue with celebrity wines is that all too often the celebrities are described as the winemakers, and the media perpetuates an image of them as having hands-on involvement. This is typically not the case; the celebrity often has nothing more to do with the winemaking process than donating his or her name—and wallet.

Of course, celebrities are used to hawk many products. The difference is that few people assume that a celebrity market-ing a brand of perfume has actually made that perfume; with wine, that assumption is often made. This likely stems from the fact that anyone can make wine. After all, home wine-making is quite common—home-perfume manufacturing, however, is not. It's not much of a stretch to imagine celebri-ties with their fingers in the fermenting tank.

But appearances are deceiving, and it is important to understand the difference between winemaking and wine marketing. A healthy dose of suspicion is required when celebrity endorse-ments and name-dropping are used to make money. In theory, a good product shouldn't need the crutch of a big name to help it on the market.

The Grape One

The puns are almost too easy. But No. 99 Estates, which falls under Wayne Gretzky's extensive business portfolio, would have you believe that it is a serious venture. Its wines, made by the winemakers at Creekside Winery in Niagara, were first released in 2007. The first wines available, a Merlot, a Chardonnay and an icewine, were generally well received by the public, well enough that Gretzky launched his own winery, No. 99 Estate Winery, in 2007.

Although hardcore wine lovers might be slightly put off by the entrance of hockey players into Canada's wine industry, there's no begrudging Gretzky's use of the winery's proceeds—everything goes to the Wayne Gretzky Foundation, which helps provide less-fortunate youth with the opportunity to play hockey. And, really, I'm sure there are a few wine buffs out there who appreciate being able to buy wine and season tickets on the same website.

DID YOU  KNOW?

Gretzky isn't the only NHL star with a passion for wine. Retired Canadian hockey player Mario Lemieux has a collection of more than 5000 bottles, mainly high-end Bordeaux from top vintages.

Booze Brother

Hollywood and the blues aren't the only entertainment ventures Dan Aykroyd has explored. Not only does he hold the rights to Patrón Spirits, the makers of ultra-premium Patrón Tequila, but Aykroyd has also invested in the wine business. He partnered up with Diamond Estates Wines & Spirits in 2005 to launch a brand of wines bearing his name.

His luck in show business has clearly held through his foray into the wine world. Dan Aykroyd wines have met with enough popularity to merit the launch of a premium reserve series of wines, which will include an icewine and several table wines made from rare varieties of grapes. In addition, Diamond Estates announced plans in 2007 to build a Dan Aykroyd winery in Niagara. The building is designed to incorporate live performances and will showcase Aykroyd's collection of entertainment memorabilia.

Snob-free Wines

Although Aykroyd clearly has a taste for the finer things in the wine (and spirits) world, his wines are made with the average person in mind. The branding is very down-to-earth, the wines marketed as "snob-free" and "full of tannins and stuff." Indeed, though these quips are designed to avoid alienating the wine novice, they are so self-effacing that they could, ironically, alienate bona fide wine snobs. Not that this is necessarily a bad thing.

DID YOU KNOW?

Dan Aykroyd isn't just into wine and tequila. He recently launched his own vodka, Crystal Head, so named because it's bottled in a glass skull.

Sympathy for the Devil

Okay, so they aren't technically Canadian, but they are involved in the Canadian wine industry. The Rolling Stones already had a series of wines marketed under their name, when they added a Canadian icewine to the playbill. Sympathy for the Devil, an icewine made from Pinot Noir, is made by Ex Nihilo Vineyards in the Okanagan Valley. The wine is the brainchild of Ex Nihilo owner Jeff Harder, who was inspired by sampling the Rolling Stones' Cabernet Sauvignon at a dinner hosted by the band. To put his dream into motion, Harder enlisted the aid of Martin Erlichman of Celebrity Cellars, a California company that designs celebrity wines. With Erlichman's help, Harder created a Canadian chapter of Celebrity Cellars, which debuted with the Rolling Stones' Pinot Noir icewine. The portfolio has since expanded to include another icewine, made from Riesling, and a red Bordeaux blend named Satisfaction.

DID YOU KNOW?

Celebrity Cellars also sells wines named for Madonna, KISS, Celine Dion and Barbra Streisand.

Taking a Swing

Am I the only one tempted to add a *d* every time I see the phrase "Weir Wines?" Okay, bad joke, but I'm sure I'm not the only one who's thought of this. Canadian PGA golfer and

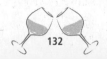

2003 Masters Tournament champion Mike Weir first released his own wine label, Mike Weir Estate Winery, in 2005. Two wines were offered, a Chardonnay and a Cabernet-Merlot, both made from 100-percent-Ontario-grown fruit. The wines were initially made at Creekside Winery in Ontario—maker of Wayne Gretzky's wines—and were quick to garner tremendous popularity across the country.

DID YOU KNOW?

In only three years, annual sales of Mike Weir's wines grew to more than 30,000 cases from 5000 cases.

Charting a New Course

Late in 2008, Mike Weir Wine Ltd. announced a change in direction for the wines through a partnership with Château des Charmes, a renowned Canadian winery. All Weir Wines are now made by the Château, which should mean a noticeable step up in quality. Château des Charmes, a pioneer of the Canadian wine industry, has not only been producing award-winning wines for more than 30 years but the company also owns one of the largest premium vineyards in the country, with almost 121 hectares of vines. Net proceeds from the sales of Weir Wines still go to the Mike Weir Foundation, which was established to advance the physical, emotional and educational welfare of Canadian children.

Another major development in the Weir Wine enterprise is the construction of the Mike Weir Winery. The winery complex will be located on the Niagara Parkway, adjacent to the 70-year-old Whirlpool Golf Course—tasters can sip wine after a long day on the green (or in the sand trap, if they visited the winery before the golf course). The facility will also feature a retail store, restaurant, vineyard and Mike Weir gallery.

HOME WINEMAKING

Nation of Home Vintners

Chances are good that every Canadian knows at least one person who makes wine in his or her basement. Uncle Bob or Aunt May's concoctions might not win any awards, but there's no denying the popularity of this pursuit. In fact, Canada holds the record for the country with the largest home-winemaking market, dwarfing all other nations by a large degree.

Booming Basement Wine

Home winemaking has been a common pursuit of many Canadians for decades. In 1976, home winemakers used some 4500 to 5400 tonnes of Canadian grapes and a whopping 78,000 tonnes of California grapes in their pursuit. But this was only the start of a serious boom in home winemaking. During the 1980s and 1990s, sales of home winemaking equipment soared. Just before the turn of the last century, industry leaders estimated that, in Canada, wine-kit sales increased tenfold over the previous decade, to approximately US$181 million annually. That number is huge, making Canada a veritable home-winemaking behemoth.

U-Vints

Marking a major milestone in Canadian home winemaking was the establishment of U-Vints (similar to U-Brews), store-front businesses that allow customers to use wine kits to make wine on site and then take it home for personal consumption. In 1989, there were four U-Vints in Ontario. By 1999, that number had grown to 640. In addition to offering the facilities necessary for making wine, U-Vints also sell personal wine-making kits and all the supplies necessary for making wine at home. British Columbia and Québec also have similar facilities.

DID YOU KNOW?

U-Vints account for 25 percent of the home winemaking market in Canada.

Retail Heaven

For the three-quarters of Canadian home winemakers who make their product at home, specialty retail stores provide their bread and butter. Throughout Canada are more than 350 retail stores offering winemaking equipment. Almost half of these are in Québec—once again, the French have proven their unquestioned devotion to fermentation. These retail stores offer a mind-boggling selection of materials, and the consumer can choose from dozens of types of wine. Home winemaking is so common in Canada that a lot of the mundane supplies, such as labels and corks, are even sold in grocery stores.

Taking Homebrew Seriously

Further proof of the size of Canada's home-winemaking industry is the level of organization within the field. The Amateur Winemakers of Canada (AWC) is the national coordinating body for amateur winemakers in Canada. It works with the provincial home winemaking associations to develop and share knowledge with all members participating in the hobby. AWC was established in the late 1960s by John G. Armstrong.

One of the most important events for the AWC is the annual home-winemaking competition. The first competition was held in 1971, and Gary Lucier of Windsor, Ontario, became the first Canadian Grand Champion. To participate, all wines must be judged at the provincial level before proceeding to the national competition. The winner receives an engraved golden key—the symbol of the AWC—along with the satisfaction and notoriety that comes with being titled "Grand Champion."

Booze Bureaucracy

One of the signs of growth in any industry is the formation of organizations to regulate it (we live in a bureaucratic world, after all). The Canadian Home Wine Trade Association (CHWTA) was formed in 1994 by the manufacturers of wine and beer kits. Its purpose includes educating and informing the media and other industry players about the importance of the industry, setting standards for kits in compliance with federal acts and regulations and resolving any issues and conflicts of interest that might arise.

The Stigma of Homebrew

Along with the huge number of enthusiastic home winemakers in Canada apparently comes an equal number of pessimists. The bottle of homemade wine is a much-maligned object, often for good reason. The industry's spokespeople and home winemakers alike will tell you that their $3 bottles of wine taste like $10 bottles. But wine is inherently subjective—and they forget that there are many bottles of bad $10 commercial wine.

Granted, it's hard to argue against the value of a $3 homemade wine that tastes like a bottle of bad $10 commercial wine, especially in times of economic turmoil. And some of that homemade wine must be decent—maybe even pretty good. Still, many wine lovers would rather leave the winemaking to the professionals and will readily choose beer over homemade wine. Ultimately, it all comes down to personal preference.

WonderWine (That Isn't Really Wine)

WonderWine allows consumers to make "wine" quickly and easily. Perhaps too easily—you can even make wine in a pop bottle! WonderWine is the brainchild of Donald Pilla, an Ontario accountant, who managed to evaporate wine and isolate the chemical constituents of the residue. Combining these compounds with yeast culture produces a wine powder, which is sold to the customer along with instructions to add water and sugar and set aside for 28 days.

In *Wines and Vines*, a British publication, the Wine Society reportedly described WonderWine as tasting "nothing like grape, more like a sour apple." European Economic Community regulations state that WonderWine cannot be called wine, because only a product made from freshly picked grapes can be called wine. Despite WonderWine's dubious quality, in 1978 (the year it was invented), sales are said to have topped $1 million in Canada, and the business is still in operation.

Artsy Wine

Stanley F. Anderson has been called the "Johnny Appleseed" of home winemaking. Anderson has taught thousands how to make wine. He has published several books on the subject, including *The Art of Making Wine* and *The Advanced Winemaker's Practical Guide*. In 1959, Anderson founded Wine-Art Sales Ltd., a retail chain for home vintners, in Vancouver. For years, the store was a staple of the industry, providing novice and veteran home winemakers with the tools and resources necessary to pursue their craft.

DID YOU KNOW?

Vancouver city police tried to close the first Wine-Art store, because selling yeast in conjunction with winemaking equipment was considered tantamount to selling wine—and under provincial law, unlicensed stores cannot sell alcoholic beverages.

CANADIAN GRAPES

A Different Species

Canada is home to several species of native grapes; the most common are *Vitis labrusca* and *Vitis riparia*. Several hybrid varieties, made from crosses between different grape species, are also grown and made into wine. However, all the common wine-producing grapes—Cabernet Sauvignon, Merlot, Chardonnay and Pinot Noir, for example—belong to the *Vitis vinifera* species. Undisputedly the noblest of grapes, *vinifera* varieties are the best for making wine. But well into the 1980s, winemakers believed they couldn't survive Canada's severe winters. Instead, they relied on the native varieties. This was the main reason why our industry lagged for so many years—there are marked differences between species, and Canada's native grapes make decidedly inferior wine.

DID YOU KNOW?

There are still a number of unidentified grape varieties growing in vineyards throughout Canada. Grapevines are constantly mutating and producing new strains, and, until DNA research identifies them, they remain "mystery grapes."

This Wine Smells Like…Wet Dog?

Taste is the biggest difference between *vinifera* grapes and other grape species. Wine made from *labrusca* and other hybrid varieties has a distinctly musky aroma. This quality is caused by two chemical compounds, methyl anthranilate and O-amino acetothenone. These compounds naturally reside in the grapes and produce that foxy flavour when fermented.

The foxy quality is most prominent in *labrusca* wines, though it is still detectable in the hybrids. Most find this smell difficult to describe, though all agree that, after you've sniffed it once, you'll never forget it. It's akin to the aroma of grape jelly; more colourful descriptors include wet dog or agitated fox. Needless to say, unlike a person bearing the same descriptor, "foxy" is not a taste one wants to experience in a wine—unless you happen to be eating a peanut butter sandwich. Or you really like dogs.

Jug Wines

Only a few decades ago, most Canadian wines found in liquor stores were made from native varieties. To combat the off-putting foxy taste, the wines were also all sweetened and fortified, some containing as much as 20 percent alcohol! Since then, *labrusca* wines have all but disappeared, though you can still find these "jug" wines occasionally, bottled in classy oversize plastic bottles with a loop handle on the neck, gracing bottom shelves and back corners.

The Long-lived Fox

"Foxy" has been used to describe the peculiar aroma of wines made from wild grapes for some time. In a paper written in 1866, Count Justin M. de Courtenay uses the term and also states that, at the time, the question of greatest importance to Canadian growers was to create wine without the foxy flavour. He goes on to state that "foxy" had almost become a slang expression (it certainly has, by now!) and that the grapes from the United States had more of this quality than those from Canada. This led him to the conclusion that native Canadian varieties would form the basis of North America's future wine industry. Wishful thinking perhaps, though he did hit home on a few points.

DID YOU KNOW?

Until 1971, the Okanagan's most important red grape variety was Bath, an American hybrid. Bath was the main grape used to make the then-wildly popular Baby Duck pop wine.

Creative Naming

Although they carry that pungent foxy flavour, you can't begrudge the colourful names of many *labrusca* and hybrid varieties. Himrod, Christmas Rose, Bluebell and Catawba are examples, as well as the "foxy" ladies of Isabella and Diana.

Many native grape varieties are named for their place of origin or in which they were most commonly grown, such as Delaware and Niagara. Hybrid varieties are also commonly named for their creators. Baco Noir, for example, takes its name from Maurice Baco, and Vidal is named for Jean Louis Vidal.

DID YOU KNOW?

Albert Seibel, a leading French viticulturist, produced more than 16,000 grape varieties, by crossing European varieties with native North American grapes. His grapes are known collectively as Seibel grapes.

Grapes with Natural Snowsuits

Labrusca grapes, unlike *vinifera* varieties, are winter hardy. This winter hardiness contributed to an extensive grape-breeding program that was developed in the mid-1900s and continues to this day. Scientists successfully bred several new species of grapes by crossing *vinifera* varieties with hardier *labrusca*, *riparia* and other indigenous varieties, to create hybrids with the desirable flavours and aromas of *vinifera* and the resilience to withstand Canada's winters.

DID YOU KNOW?

New hybrid varieties are being developed all the time. Several wineries in Nova Scotia have started planting "Cabernet Foch," a cross between Cabernet Sauvignon and Maréchal Foch varieties, engineered by Swiss plant breeder Valentin Blattner.

L'Acadie

L'Acadie Blanc (often shortened to simply L'Acadie) is a Nova Scotia grape variety. Not only is it the province's most widely planted grape, but it is also the most successful and is almost unique to the province—only a few pockets grow elsewhere, in New Brunswick. A hybrid, L'Acadie was bred to be winter hardy and early ripening. It was created at Ontario's Vineland Research Station in 1953 but never caught on in Niagara. It found a welcome home on the Atlantic, however, performing better than Seyval Blanc (Nova Scotia's previous champion white variety). Nova Scotia wine pioneer Roger Dial made the first L'Acadie wine in 1975. It is somewhat akin to Chardonnay, in that it can be made in two very different styles: crisp, fresh and bone dry, with flavours of apples, pears and citrus; or off-dry, with buttery, vanilla oak flavours by aging on the lees (the solid grape particles that precipitate out of a wine).

DID YOU KNOW?

L'Acadie's original name was V-53261. After making wine from this grape, Roger Dial christened it with the decidedly more romantic name L'Acadie.

Hybrids Rule

You will be hard pressed to find a 100-percent-labrusca wine on today's liquor store shelves. Don't get me wrong: this is a good thing. Native grapes simply make inferior wine, and nothing can be done about it. However, a few premium hybrid varieties are still available, and they are worth checking out—not just for a glimpse of what Canada's earlier wines were like but also to see how far they have come. Some great hybrids to try are Baco Noir, Maréchal Foch, Seyval Blanc and L'Acadie.

Maréchal Foch

Maréchal Foch is one of Canada's pioneering varieties; it replaced many *labrusca* grape varieties, such as Concord, when it was introduced in 1946 as part of a group of French hybrid grapes brought from Europe by wine pioneer Adhemar de Chaunac. Foch was developed in France's Alsace region by grape hybridizer Eugene Kulmann; its original name was Kulmann 188-2 but was changed to the more lyrical Maréchal Foch. This name honours Marshall Foch, a French general who helped negotiate armistice in World War I.

Although it lacks the sophistication of the *vinifera* varieties, Maréchal Foch is far better than the *labrusca* it replaced.

Foch, as it is commonly called, can even attain a degree of grace when made properly. Much like humans, it performs best after living for a while: younger vines make rather forgettable wine, whereas older vines can make concentrated wines redolent with aromas of black fruits and bearing a distinct gamey quality.

Although a few dedicated souls still grow the grape, for the most part, Foch languishes in obscurity. After Canada's extensive pullout program in the late 1980s, a huge portion of Foch vines was supplanted by *vinifera* varieties, and plantings have fallen steadily since then—though, in recent years, Ontario has seen a slight increase in Foch plantings. This grape will always occupy a niche market, but there is still a dedicated, albeit small, group of vintners and consumers who appreciate the uniqueness of this Canadian pioneer.

DID YOU  KNOW?

The last Canadian wine made from 100-percent-*labrusca* grapes is likely to have been from Niagara's Thomas & Vaughan winery, which, until the late 1990s, made a dessert wine from a small parcel of Catawba grapes.

Winery Profile **Quails' Gate Estate Winery**

From its humble beginnings as a farm winery in 1989, Quails' Gate has become one of the Okanagan's leading wine producers, making about 40,000 cases a year. The winery was founded by Ben and Tony Stewart, two brothers from a family of pioneer Okanagan horticulturists—their father

Winery Profile

helped plant one of the first vineyards in the southern Okanagan. Quails' Gate is famous for hiring winemakers from Down Under. A string of Australian and New Zealand winemakers has created a consistent portfolio of wines. The winery is also renowned for its Old Vines Foch, an intensely flavourful red made from the winery's 25-year-old Maréchal Foch vines. The wine has attained cult status in wine circles throughout the country.

DID YOU KNOW?

A 2007 Quails' Gate Chenin Blanc was served to U.S. President Obama during his visit to Ottawa in February 2009. Other Canadian wines gracing the list were a 2002 Stratus Vineyards Red from Niagara and a 2005 La Face Cachée de la Pomme Neige, an apple icewine from Québec.

Baco Noir

Baco Noir, another one of Canada's hybrid workhorse grapes, is an old drinking buddy of Maréchal Foch. Once quite popular and widely planted, Baco Noir has now fallen out of favour. The two varieties share similar histories: like Foch, Baco was created in France by a wine hybridizer (Maurice Baco), and it arrived in Canada at about the same time, in 1955.

Many Baco vines were torn up during the 1980s vine-pull program, though not to the same extent as Foch; Baco is still more common. Although Baco is planted in both Ontario and British Columbia, the grape has always been more prevalent in Ontario.

Henry of Pelham Family Estate Winery

Henry of Pelham is one of Niagara's benchmark producers. The winery was founded by the Speck family; Paul Speck Sr. purchased the property in 1982. With the help of his sons, Paul Jr., Daniel and Matt, Paul Sr. planted some of British Colombia's first vinifera grapes in 1984. The winery was established in 1987.

The winery is located on property that has belonged to the Speck family's ancestors since 1794. Henry Smith, son of the original owner, Nicholas Smith, built an inn on the site in 1842, which now serves as the tasting room, store and restaurant. His countenance has been immortalized on the wine labels. The winery is one of the biggest supporters of Baco Noir. In fact, Pelham's Baco is arguably the best expression of this grape to be had anywhere. A "true

☞

Winery Profile

north" wine, with woodsy, rustic flavours, it is usually quite dark in colour and fruit forward, with black fruits, berry, leather and often a gamey undercurrent. Baco isn't a long-lived wine, making it a great choice for the impatient—it is best consumed within its first five to seven years.

DID YOU KNOW?

Henry of Pelham released Canada's first VQA-approved screw-cap bottle.

Vidal

If there's one grape that proves the merit of hybrid varieties, it's Vidal Blanc—or Vidal, as it is commonly called. This grape is eminently suited to making icewine and has been at the forefront of the icewine industry since Canadians first started making this frozen nectar—Canadian vintners owe a huge amount of respect to this winter-loving berry.

Vidal is a cross of Ugni Blanc (also known as Trebbiano), a workhorse grape widely planted throughout Europe, and Seibel 4986 (a *labrusca* variety also called Rayon d'Or). It was developed in France in the 1930s by Jean Louis Vidal, a French breeder who was trying to produce grapes suitable for Cognac production. Vidal's rugged winter hardiness made it an immediate favourite in Canada's chilly wine regions.

Like many hybrids with *labrusca* parentage, Vidal has a thick skin, which is perfect for making icewine. The skin stays intact as the temperature drops, keeping the berries in good condition until it is cold enough for harvesting. Vidal is also high in acidity, making it largely unsuitable for dry table wines—unless the drinker is interested in removing a layer of tooth enamel. However, this acidity works well to balance the high sugar levels of frozen grapes; Vidal makes superbly balanced icewine.

De Chaunac

Never heard of De Chaunac? It's time to get acquainted. This grape bears the name of its creator, one of the true pioneers of the fledgling Canadian wine industry. Adhemar de Chaunac was born in France and emigrated to Canada as a young child. He worked extensively in the Canadian wine industry for much of his life, notably at Brights Wines in Niagara, where he became chief chemist in 1933 and director of research in 1944. During his tenure at Brights, de Chaunac brought 35 French hybrid varieties into Canada—including Maréchal Foch, Baco Noir and the variety that came to bear de Chaunac's own name. The introduction of these varieties, which proved to be eminently better than the *labrusca* varieties being used, marked a major milestone in Canadian wine industry.

De Chaunac has not maintained its status nor is it grown as much as other hybrids, such as Foch and Baco Noir, but you can still find pockets of vines scattered throughout eastern Canada, particularly in the neophyte wine regions of Québec and Nova Scotia.

DID YOU KNOW?

De Chaunac was originally named Seibel 9549—it was one of the thousands of grapes developed by French viticulturist Albert Seibel.

Winery Profile — Gaspereau Vineyards

Gaspereau Vineyards is Nova Scotia's smallest winery, producing approximately 2000 cases of wine per year—ironic, given that its owners, Hans Christian and Karen Jost, also operate the largest winery in the province: Jost Vineyards in the Malagash Peninsula. With such a successful business in another region, why would the Josts take up winemaking in such an isolated area? Well, practicality came first: the Josts wanted to spread their risk over a wider area—not put their all eggs in one basket, if you will. Second, Hans Christian feels that the Gaspereau has more potential as a winegrowing region than any other area in Nova Scotia. The winery has already succeeded in producing small amounts of well-made wine, mainly made from hybrid varieties. De Chaunac plays an especially important role here, and the winery makes one of Canada's best examples of the grape.

Sovereign Opal

Calona Vineyards in British Columbia is the only grower of Sovereign Opal. Technically named Summerland Selection 166, it was developed at the Summerland Research Station and was provided to growers for trial in 1976. Sovereign Opal is a cross of Golden Muscat and Maréchal Foch, with fresh floral characters from the Muscat. A lively wine, it is best consumed in its youth.

Calona's winemaker, Howard Soon, makes his Sovereign Opal off-dry, because the grape's naturally high acidity can be a little too bracing if the wine is dry.

A WINEMAKER'S SPICE RACK: THE IMPORTANCE OF OAK

An Oak Finish

Oak is like a winemaker's spice rack. Just as a chef uses spices to add layers to a meal, a winemaker uses different types of oak to add layers to a wine. This is usually done during the aging process, after the wine has been fermented; the wine is stored in barrels for several months or even years before being bottled. However, winemakers can also add oak influence during the fermentation process, by fermenting the wine in oak barrels or by adding oak chips, powder and staves to the fermenting wine.

Oak Experiments

French and American oaks are most commonly used in the wine industry. However, Canadian winemakers have experimented with all kinds of oak, including local Canadian oak. Other types of wood that have also been used by Canadian vintners, albeit on a much smaller scale, include acacia, chestnut, pine and redwood.

Bring on the Barrels

Canadian oak is new to the wine industry and has only been used to age wine since the early 21st century. The driving force behind this innovation is a pair of amateur Canadian winemakers, Jim Hedges and Michael Risk. In 1999, a serendipitous chain of events led the two men, the former a cardiac surgical assistant and the latter a retired geology professor, to experiment with aging wine in Canadian oak barrels. After helping clear away some mature oak trees from Hedges' sister's woodlot, the two men wondered if they could make wine barrels from the wood. Because there were no professional barrel-makers (known as coopers) in Canada at that time, Hedges and Risk drove a bundle of hand-cut wooden staves to a cooperage in Arkansas. They returned a few days later with three miniature barrels, and thus began their experimentation with aging wine in Canadian oak. They have since created Canadian Oak Cooperage, a company in Niagara that sells wine barrels made from Canadian oak.

Following their first experiments with Canadian oak barrels, Hedges and Risk convinced Ontario's Lailey Vineyards to do a test run of wine aged in Canadian oak. The first commercial wine to be aged in Canadian oak was Lailey's 2001 Chardonnay, which was well received by both wine writers and imbibers alike. After this, a handful of Canadian wineries began experimenting with the barrels, and they caught on quickly—dozens of wineries now use Canadian oak barrels to age their wines.

DID YOU KNOW?

Other Canadian producers that have used Canadian oak to age their wines include Burrowing Owl, Henry of Pelham, Inniskillin, Jackson-Triggs and Daniel Lenko.

BC Barrels

At the opposite end of the country, in the Okanagan Valley, Cal Craik started Okanagan Barrel Works in 2001, with the intent to refurbish wine barrels for the thriving British Columbia wine industry. However, within the first year, Craik realized that most of his customers weren't commercial wineries, they were home winemakers. To meet the demand, Okanagan Barrel Works sells various sizes of small barrels (5, 10, 20, 50 and 100 litres), which are perfect for the home winemaker. The cooperage also sells the standard 225-litre barrel for use in commercial wineries and offers other useful tools for small wineries and home winemakers, such as glassware, bottling supplies and lab equipment. Craik even runs an in-house custom toasting service, in which winemakers can have their oak chips or staves toasted to their specification.

Distinctly Canadian

Most Canadian oak comes from forests in southern Ontario. These trees belong to the species *Quercus alba*—the same species as American oak. However, Canadian oak is tighter-grained than its American counterpart, because of the cooler growing climate, and doesn't contribute the same degree of flavour components to wines aged in it. Canadian oak is distinct from French and American oak. Many feel that it occupies the middle ground between the heady vanilla flavours imparted by American oak and the subtle, cigar-box aromas of French oak. Others detect a decidedly herbaceous undercurrent to the wines, with flavours such as dill and fresh green herbs—some even claim to smell marijuana!

However, more time is required before a thorough knowledge of the flavours of Canadian oak is attained; the wines aged in this oak are still very young. It will be interesting to see the range of flavours that appear in Canadian oak wines that have been cellared for several years.

French Oak

French oak is the world standard by which all other oak is judged. Most French oak comes from the central forests of Allier, Nevers and Tronçais and from the northern Vosges forest near the region of Alsace. With more than four million hectares of the best wine-barrel species, *Quercus petraea* and *Quercus robur*, France is by far the largest supplier of wine-barrel oak in Europe. More than 200,000 French oak barrels are made every year, most of which are sold to the United States. The French have also been very diligent with forestry management, so French oak is available in viable commercial quantities every year.

French oak's smaller pores and tighter grain impart a subtler flavour to wine than does North American oak, with hints of spice, cigar box, toast and smoke.

DID YOU KNOW?

Almost a quarter of France is covered in forest, a third of which is oak.

American Oak

Quercus alba, the species of oak used to make American wine barrels, grows mostly in forests located in the eastern part of the United States. Although oak forests grow throughout the rest of the country, especially in the northwest, they are composed of species unsuitable for barrels. Between 150,000 and 200,000 American oak barrels are sold to producers in the United States alone. American oak is also widely used throughout Canada, Spain, Australia and South America.

American oak has larger pores and a looser grain than French oak, so it imparts a stronger flavour to wines aged in it. The most common flavour associated with American oak is vanillin—not unlike the pungent aroma of vanilla extract. This type of oak can also make wine more astringent and is therefore best used with powerful red wines; lighter-bodied wines are overpowered if they spend too much time in American oak.

Acacia

Domaine de Chaberton Estate Winery is the first—and so far, only—winery in Canada to release an acacia-aged wine. Its 1994 Chardonnay was aged for several months in acacia barrels. Acacia has been used to age wines for centuries in Hungary and other parts of Eastern Europe but is fairly obscure throughout the rest of the world. Acacia gives wine aromas of honey and flowers, and because it doesn't impart tannins or vanilla flavours, like other types of oak, it can be used to age light, delicate wines. Unfortunately, Domaine de Chaberton seems to be the only winery to be experimenting with acacia; perhaps we'll see more Canadian vintners trying these rare barrels in the future.

DID YOU KNOW?

Aging in acacia barrels gives wine a deep golden hue.

Eastern European Oak

In the past, the forests of Eastern Europe were extremely important sources of oak. However, political turmoil, combined with the environmental and economic damage suffered during World War II, has curtailed the availability of much of this region's oak supply. The fact that the forests throughout most of the countries in Eastern Europe have been poorly managed hasn't helped, either. Because Canada's wine industry is so young, few Canadian wines have been aged in Eastern European oak.

The Flavour Isn't Free

Wine barrels aren't cheap. In fact, they are one of the winery's biggest annual expenses. French oak is by far the most expensive, sometimes reaching double the price of American oak. The price for a standard French oak barrel is approximately US$600; American oak goes for slightly less than US$300. Canadian oak is also quite expensive, perhaps because it occupies such a niche market, and the supply is not plentiful. A standard barrel of Canadian oak goes for about US$750.

Barrel Back-ups

Because oak barrels are so expensive, many wineries cannot afford to use them every year or for every wine. Winemakers must use a variety of other methods to impart that highly desirable oak influence to their wines, such as using oak chips, staves and barrel inserts. These materials are usually added to the wine while it is fermenting; in this volatile state, the wine picks up the oak influence much more quickly. The oak material is then filtered out or removed at the end of the process.

Although these cheaper methods of adding oak flavour certainly do the job, wines made in this way are often scorned as inferior. Many feel that the flavour is "cheaper" and that there is no substitute for months of aging in oak barrels. Others argue that these methods are actually more environmentally friendly, because they employ scraps that would otherwise be discarded. It is ultimately up to the consumer to decide which method he or she prefers—but there's no denying that these wines will continue to be produced, so long as oak barrels remain at their current prices.

DID YOU  KNOW?

The oak chips used in winemaking are usually about the size of a cashew—though, on occasion, they can be as small as pencil shavings.

ENJOYING THE FRUITS OF OUR LABOUR

Animals Gone Wild

Think humans are the only creatures that enjoy the fruits of a vineyard? Think again. A well-manicured vineyard, its ripe bunches of grapes dangling within easy reach just below the trellising, is a veritable buffet for all manner of woodland creatures. Vineyard workers are often alerted to the onset of harvest season not by their own measurements but by seeing the local wildlife take a sizeable chunk out of the harvest! Everything from birds and bears to wasps and deer leave their mark on an unprotected vineyard.

Winged Predators

Most people, especially city dwellers, cherish the sound of happily chirping birds. But to vineyard workers, those chirps aren't the sounds of a cheery summer afternoon—they are cries of war. Birds are one of the biggest threats to any vineyard—an undisturbed flock can strip a vineyard of several acres of grapes in one afternoon.

Starlings and robins are the major culprits. Although their eating habits vary, the end result is the same: a serious deficit in the grape harvest. Robins are like your elderly great aunt—they're dainty eaters that peck just enough grapes to get the taste before moving on to another bunch. Unfortunately, the juice from the damaged grapes runs over the rest of them and quickly rots, spoiling the entire bunch. Starlings are more voracious than your 15-year-old nephew. These birds will systematically chow through bunch after bunch, eating every single berry. At the end of their feeding rampage, there is nothing left but the naked stems.

Fighting the Flocks

Because birds pose such a big threat, every vineyard must employ some form of control. The most common are scare guns, colloquially known as "bird bangers." These giant air cannons go off periodically with a giant thumping noise, scattering any birds that might be dining al fresco. Although air cannons are often enough to deter starlings, robins are, shall we say, not as bright as their cousins. Robins are not only undaunted by the bangers, some have even been reported to perch on the edge of the guns!

Scarecrows, which are also commonly used to stave off the damage done by birds, are cheap and fairly effective—though they need to be moved around the vineyard regularly, to keep the birds guessing. Netting is also used and is highly effective, but its price tag is prohibitive for many wine producers.

Birds have driven many vineyard workers to their wits' end, and some have resorted to more unusual tactics. Playing recordings of starling distress calls has proven quite effective—good thing birds don't have opposable thumbs to change the station. Other wineries have floated helium balloons over their vineyards, with hawk replicas dangling underneath. Still others have simply thrown up their hands and listened when they were told to go fly a kite—with an image of a hawk or other raptor on it.

DID YOU KNOW?

Inniskillin attempted to make icewine in 1983, but the entire harvest was eaten by birds. The winery made its first icewine a year later, with the help of bird netting.

Annual Arrivals

In the untamed Okanagan, one of the first signs of harvest is the annual arrival of black bears in the vineyards. If left undisturbed, the bears can ravage a vineyard, leaving nothing behind but a steaming pile of scat—composed completely of grape skins.

DID YOU  KNOW?

One adult bear can eat as much as 135 kilograms of grapes in one night.

Picky Palates

Bears have their flavour preferences, just like any wine enthusiast, preferring grapes that become sweet and fragrant early in the season—Muscat is a perennial favourite. Unlike birds, which only eat the fruit and leave the vines intact, bears are more zealous eaters. One swipe of a massive paw rips the bunches down, doing serious damage to both vine and trellising; bears also have no consideration for irrigation lines and other vineyard infrastructure in their lusty feeding.

Smarter than the Average Bear

Although they are not as common as birds, bears are just as tricky to banish from the vineyard. The first line of defense, and the least harmful, is catch and release. Vineyards are provided with live traps, which are successful some of the time. All too often, the bears prove themselves too smart to be caught in a metal box. After all, with acres upon acres of dinner just a paw swipe away, the trap's bait must look pretty unappetizing.

If the catch-and-release tactic doesn't work, attempts can be made to scare the bears away, either by firing warning shots when bears are encountered on a grape rampage or through other activities that impede their foraging, such as installing fences, clearing nearby forested areas and using scare devices such as strobe lights, loud music, air cannons and scarecrows. Occasionally, and only when there is no other alternative, those shots are no longer just a warning…and bear winds up on the dinner menu at the winery's restaurant.

Party Crashers

Although most vineyard workers undoubtedly worry more about the damage wasps do to them than to the grapes, these insects can also leave their destructive mark on a field of plump fruit. Wasps puncture the grape's skin and suck out the pulp, leaving nothing behind but the skins, dangling lifelessly from the stems like a bunch of deflated party balloons.

Buzz Kill

Fortunately, wasps are one of the easier grape predators to combat. Destroying the nest, though this admittedly comes with the attendant hazard of a hundred angry stingers pointed your way, usually solves the problem. Once the nests are destroyed, the area is monitored, so that new nests can be wiped out before they grow too large. Growers can also prevent wasps from relocating in the vineyard by hanging fake nests throughout the area—because wasps are territorial, they won't move into an area already occupied by a hive.

DID YOU  KNOW?

Wasps aren't the only insects that can wreck a vineyard. In Niagara, 2001 became known as the "ladybug harvest," when an infestation of ladybugs contaminated several wines with a compound called pyrazine—making the wine smell like peanuts.

Vine Chewers

Bambi and his colleagues might be cute, but they certainly have no respect for a hardworking Canadian grape grower. Anyone who has had a garden in the country will know how damaging these critters can be. Deer usually don't go for the grapes first; they prefer to munch on the tender young vine shoots in the spring, which is much more damaging than eating the grapes. Eating the shoots retards the vine's growth for the rest of the season, reducing the crop significantly—if it doesn't kill the vine outright.

Taming Bambi

Wire fences are a common and fairly effective way of preventing deer from getting into the vineyard. However, because deer can jump quite high, the fence needs to be tall, so this isn't always an affordable option. Odour repellents can also be employed; small bags filled with offensive material (to a deer's sensibilities) are hung in the vines and in the trees around the perimeter of the vineyard. Repellents include moth flakes, soap and blood meal (which would probably repel the average person, as well). Another successful repellent is, strangely enough, human hair. A small sack filled with hair, obtained from the friendly neighbourhood barbershop, often keeps the deer away. Replacing the hair monthly keeps the scent fresh.

However, if other food sources are limited or nonexistent, nothing will prevent hungry deer from trying to get at a field of food, and sometimes vineyard workers must resort to permanent tactics to eliminate some of the troublesome animals, especially if the local population is high.

DID YOU  KNOW?

Vancouver Island's Blue Grouse Estate Winery has such a problem with deer that the entire vineyard is surrounded by an electric fence.

BRITISH COLUMBIA

A Fruity Beginning

BC's first wines were made from loganberries, which only grow in certain tucked-away corners of the world. The southern region of Vancouver Island is an ideal location, and loganberries grow in abundance here. The BC wine industry made loganberry wine for decades, until a disease wiped out most of the bushes in the 1960s.

DID YOU  KNOW?

No one really knows what loganberries are. They are most commonly believed to be a cross between a raspberry and a blackberry, created in 1881 by American horticulturist J.H. Logan—but this is not certain.

Growers' Wine Company

Growers' Wine Company was formed in 1922 with the initial purpose of processing BC's surplus loganberries. The company was located in Victoria, on Vancouver Island. Five years later, Victoria Wineries (British Columbia) Ltd. opened its doors and also began making loganberry wine. However, although there were certainly enough berries to make into wine, demand for loganberry wines was not high, and Victoria merged with Growers' in 1932. For decades, in response to the popularity of port-style wines, Growers' made wines that were fortified to about 20 percent alcohol, and the company continued to produce loganberry wine well into the 1960s.

Growers' was acquired by Ontario-based Jordan wines in 1973, and the Growers' winery in Victoria was closed; the new company was named Jordan & Ste. Michelle. In 1986, Jordan &

Ste. Michelle was purchased by Brights, which merged with Cartier-Inniskillin in 1993 to form Vincor International. The Growers' label still exists as a brand in the Vincor portfolio.

Winery Profile — Elephant Island Orchard Wines

Situated in the Naramata Bench of the Okanagan Valley, Elephant Island isn't really an island, and there aren't any elephants there. It doesn't have anything to do with the eponymous island in Antarctica, either. Elephant Island Orchard Wines was founded in 1999 by Miranda and Del Halladay, in partnership with Miranda's grandmother, Catherine Wisnicki. The winemaker, Christine Leroux, trained at the prestigious L'Institut d'Oenologie de Bordeaux in France. Elephant Island crafts wines from a plethora of fruits in a variety of styles, though the majority are dry table wines. Since its inception, the winery's strategy has been to make fruit wines that are as food-friendly as grape wines.

DID YOU KNOW?

There are more than 100 fruit wineries in Canada. Fruit wines are made in all 10 provinces; grape wines are only made in four.

Modern Fruit Wine

British Columbia is home to 20 fruit wineries, cideries and honey wineries (meaderies). Some of these operations only produce fruit wines; others make both grape and fruit wines. Most of these wineries are scattered throughout the main wine-producing regions of the Okanagan and Similkameen valleys, and the fruit grows alongside the grapes. Although a few wineries harvest wild fruit, most of them make wine from orchard-grown fruit.

Bumper Crops

British Columbia is blessed with a climate that can sustain all types of fruit, providing fruit winemakers with plenty of options. Almost every fruit winery makes wines with traditional favourites, such as apples, pears, cherries, blackberries and peaches, but just as many wineries experiment with more unusual fruits. You can find British Columbia fruit wines made from rhubarb, kiwis, quinces and even pumpkins. Honey is also widely used to make wine. Although honey wine (also known as mead) is not technically made from fruit, it is usually classified as a fruit wine.

Winery Profile **Forbidden Fruit Winery**

Forbidden Fruit's boutique winery is located on Ven'Amour Organic Farms, along the banks of the Similkameen River at ☞

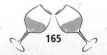

Winery Profile

the southern end of the Similkameen Valley. The farm has been under organic production since its inception in 1977 and became certified organic in 1984, the year organic certification was implemented in BC.

Fruit-wine pioneers Steve Venables and Kim Brind'Amour started the winery in 1981 and make wines from apricots, cherries, peaches, pears, plums and several species of apples. Much of the fruit comes from their own organic orchard, though they also source fruit from other areas of the Similka-meen and Okanagan valleys. The couple has also established a nature reserve on their land, and the winery is a conservation partner with the Land Conservancy of BC, which helps protect the area's rare, old-growth riparian forest and desert steppes.

THE PRAIRIES

Land of the Cottage Winery

Although Prairie winters are undisputedly cold—too cold for wine grapes—a few pockets in Manitoba, Saskatchewan and Alberta produce an abundance of fruit. However, until very recently, prairie fruit wines were almost all homemade. Commercial fruit wineries only began appearing in the last decade, or so, when provincial governments began recognizing the potential of the fruit-wine industry. The Alberta government passed a law allowing cottage wineries in 2005; Saskatchewan and Manitoba established fruit wineries in the late 1990s and early 2000s, respectively.

DID YOU KNOW?

Manitoba's D.D. Leobard Winery had to fill out a brewery application in 2000 because the provincial government had not yet created any forms for winery licensing.

Innovative Ingredients
Wines in the Prairie provinces are made from a wide variety of fruit, many of which are not immediately familiar to outsiders. These include wild cranberries, elderberries, Saskatoon berries, highbush cranberries and chokecherries. Some enterprising wineries have even made wine from such ingredients as alfalfa, birch sap and rose petals!

DID YOU  KNOW?

Saskatoon berries go by many names, depending on where you live. The berry is known as the Saskatoon in western Canada, but it is known as Juneberry, serviceberry and shadbush in various eastern provinces.

Small Size, Big Dreams

The majority of fruit wineries in the Prairies tend to be small operations, much smaller in scale than the behemoths found elsewhere in Canada. Production from Prairie fruit wineries, on average, ranges from a few hundred to 2000 cases of fruit wine a year. In contrast, fruit wineries in BC and Ontario often make more than 5000 cases a year, and some produce upwards of 10,000 cases in huge production facilities. Prairie fruit wines are made in sheds, barns and even old trailers! Producers often operate in conjunction with U-pick orchardists; leftover and cosmetically challenged fruit is used to make wine. (You might not want to sink your teeth into a misshapen apple, but it makes a perfectly good bottle of apple wine!)

DID YOU  KNOW?

In 2009, the Alberta Gaming and Liquor Commission passed a law allowing cottage wineries to sell their products and hold tastings in Alberta Agriculture–approved farmers' markets.

Winery Profile en Santé Winery

The Chrapko family, owners of en Santé Winery, are pioneers of the Alberta fruit-wine industry. After several years of lobbying his local MLA, the late Victor Chrapko helped bring about the provincial law allowing cottage wineries. An amateur winemaker for several decades, Chrapko was a hog farmer who switched gears completely in the mid-1990s, planting an extensive apple and tree-fruit orchard. Since his passing, his daughters have taken over production. En Santé, located in east-central Alberta, near the town of Two Hills, is the only completely organic fruit orchard and winery in the entire province. Its wines are made from apples, raspberries, wild cherries, highbush cranberries, rhubarb and even alfalfa. Working in conjunction with a small honeybee operation, the winery also produces a delicious mead.

ONTARIO

Scattered Among the Grapes

Although Ontario's fruit-wine industry is dwarfed by the grape-wine industry, its producers take their wines just as seriously. There are roughly two dozen fruit wineries in Ontario, most solely producing fruit wine, though a few make grape wines as well. As in British Columbia, Ontario fruit is grown in the same areas as grapes—though many fruits (apples and berries, especially) are hardier and can grow in regions where grapes fail to thrive.

Putting Things in Order

The most organized of the provincial fruit-wine makers, Ontario's producers established Fruit Wines of Ontario, a chapter of the Fruit Wines of Canada organization, in 2000. The association was established to maintain and promote quality standards across the fruit-wine industry. Fruit Wines of Canada, modelled on the VQA, is the first of its kind in the world. Fruit wines bearing the association's QC (Quality Certified) designation on their labels have met the association's quality standards.

Leading the Pack

Although dozens of individuals have contributed to the growing success of Canadian fruit wines, Jim Warren stands apart as one of the most influential. Warren, a consulting winemaker who has made both grape and fruit wines in Ontario for decades, has won numerous awards and accolades over the years. He was voted Winemaker of the Year in 1996 and was the Ontario Amateur Winemaker Champion and Canadian Amateur Winemaker Champion three times. Because of his extensive experience working with fruit wines, Warren was also instrumental in establishing the Fruit Wines of Ontario association and framing Canada's national fruit winemaking laws.

Winery Profile — Archibald Orchards and Estate Winery

Archibald Orchards and Estate Winery owner and operator Fred Archibald might declare himself too scared to grow grapes, but there's no denying his fearless expertise in crafting an array of striking fruit wines. Most of Archibald's wines are made from apples, though the winery also sources fruits and berries from neighbouring farms. Archibald insists that his apple wines express *terroir*, just like grape wines, and can be distinguished from apple wines made elsewhere.

Archibald's wines run the gamut of styles, from very dry to extremely sweet. The winery has also experimented with aging apple wines in oak and with making wine from frozen apples, to no small degree of success; Archibald Orchards and Estate Winery was the breakaway champion of the 2003 National Fruit Wineries of Canada Competition and was named Winery of the Year.

QUÉBEC AND THE MARITIMES

The Cider Houses Rule

Québec's fruit wines, specifically apple cider, are far more consistent in quality than its grape wines. In fact, Québec's apple orchards outnumber vineyards by a significant percentage, and the province makes almost as much apple cider as it does grape wine. (Québec also produces many other apple products in addition to cider.) Most cider is produced in the apple-heavy regions south of Montréal. Cider is made from dozens of apple varieties; like grapes, apples are a diverse species—though you might only be familiar with a handful of grocery store varieties. Québec cideries also make cider in many different styles, including sparkling, dessert and even ice cider.

DID YOU  KNOW?

Québec wineries also make fruit wine from stone fruits, berries and honey, but these are recent developments, and cider is still dominant.

Cider's Ups and Downs

Cider production in Québec goes back several centuries to 1650, when Sulpician priests planted apple trees and built a cider press on the slopes of Mount Royal, the mountain in the middle of present-day Montréal. By 1850, several producers in this area had become successful enough to see their cider shipped as far away as the Caribbean.

However, the cider industry began to wane in the 1900s. A gross oversight in the establishment of Québec's liquor laws in 1921 resulted in cider's exclusion from the regulatory framework. Farmers continued making cider and selling it locally, until an even greater obstacle presented itself a few decades later, when the province began to favour the licensing of large commercial producers—effectively shutting down most farm cideries. Québec's cider renaissance didn't come until 1998, when the government created a licence for "artisanal" cider. In just a short time, the number of cideries grew quickly.

Winery Profile — Domaine Pinnacle

For proof of Québec's supremacy in the cider world, look no further than Domaine Pinnacle. Domaine Pinnacle is run by Charles Crawford and his wife, Susan, who knew next to nothing about running a cider mill when they purchased a 175-hectare orchard in 2000. They were fast learners, however, and Domaine Pinnacle is now one of the biggest-selling brands in Québec, garnering worldwide

☞

recognition and winning more than 22 gold medals in national and international competitions. The product lineup consists entirely of ice cider, including an interesting cream ice cider—it's like the Irish Cream of the cider world!

DID YOU KNOW?

Many Québec cideries have experimented with making ice cider, which is modelled on icewine. The apples must be picked after the first autumn frost, though some producers leave them on the tree until they are completely frozen.

Maritime Fruit Wines

Nova Scotia, along with the rest of the Maritimes, also produces a lot of fruit wine. In fact, fruit wines outnumber grape wines here by a large ratio, because there is a plentiful supply of fruit that can survive the area's often-unforgiving climate. Although the rolling hills of the Atlantic provinces are buried in snow for a good portion of the year, a profusion of berries carpets the landscape in the summer months. Here, berries that aren't found anywhere else in the world produce truly unique wines. All manner of fruit, including blueberries, apples, bilberries, wild raspberries, partridgeberries, bakeapples and cherries, are used to make wine.

Winery Profile — Rodrigues Winery

Although it might seem incongruous, Canada's largest exclusively fruit winery is located in Markland, Newfoundland. Rodrigues Winery's annual production tops 25,000 cases—unlike the vast majority of fruit wineries, this is no small operation. Established in 1993, the winery makes Canada's first certified kosher wines, and fruit vodkas and brandies are made in an on-site distillery. Rodrigues' fruit is pesticide-free and hand-picked. Rodrigues has undergone an extensive expansion since 1998, and the company is expanding their overseas market; its wines are even available in Japan!

MEAD

The World's Oldest Drink

Mead, commonly referred to as honey wine, is made from the fermentation of honey. It is a very old drink—in fact, it might be the first alcoholic beverage made by humans; evidence suggests that it originated in Africa some 20,000 to 40,000 years ago. Archaeological evidence has shown that mead was an important part of ancient Roman, Nordic and European cultures.

Abuzz with Potential

Although the Canadian mead industry is still quite small, the recent popularity of fruit wines, combined with Canada's resounding international success with icewine, suggests that mead has a rosy future. Meaderies are poised on the cusp of rapid expansion, and a few Canadian entrepreneurs have already laid the groundwork for the years to come.

Winery Profile — Intermiel

Founded in 1976 by Christian and Viviane Macle, Intermiel is one of Canada's older mead houses. It is also one of Québec's major honey producers, with about 2000 hives. The Macles began making honey wine in 1991 and haven't looked back since. The meadery makes honey wine from several different kinds of honey and from blends of honey and fruit, including raspberries, blueberries and even rose petals. Almost all of Intermiel's meads are dry enough to be paired with food, and many of their sweet wines make fine pairings with desserts.

DID YOU KNOW?

Québec has more than a dozen wineries making honey wine.

NOT YOUR TYPICAL WINERY

Les Garagistes

Think of wineries, and the great châteaux of France and castles of Germany probably spring to mind. These large, historical estates are thought to be the classic houses of wine production, yet they account for only a small percentage of the world's winemaking facilities. Indeed, most wine is made in functional, unadorned spaces—winemaking is a science, after all. All that's needed is a space to hold the equipment; the size of the operation dictates how much room is needed. Wine can be, and is, made in garages, sheds and trailers. Wine made in small quantities in places such as these is called "garagiste wine," and its makers are garagistes. Surprisingly, the garagiste movement is quite popular in the Old World, in places such as France, Spain and Italy.

The Best of all Worlds

Although Canada is a young nation, with an even younger wine industry, it has not shied away from building structures that romanticize and mythologize wine. Canada's wine regions are home to many grand buildings that pay homage to traditional European wineries. But they also boast ultra-modern wineries, using the latest technology to maximize their functionality. And tucked alongside these are operations that fall into the garagiste style of winemaking; when driving through Niagara or the Okanagan, you might never know if that old barn, shed or cottage actually houses an award-winning winery!

Cyberspace Wine

A relatively new trend of the British Columbia wine scene is the virtual winery. You can't visit these wineries, for the simple reason that they don't physically exist. Under BC wine regulations, a winemaker can "piggyback" on a colleague's licence; he or she can legally make and bottle wine at that facility without having his or her own licence. Virtual wineries are really just a label, though a few have tasting rooms and stores, usually attached to the host's winery. Their wines are sold in private retail stores, through the Internet, by mail order or in the host's shop.

DID YOU  KNOW?

Virtual wineries aren't just an underground phenomenon—some well-known names, including Sandhill, Paradise Ranch and Desert Hills, are actually virtual wineries.

ARCHITECTURAL WINERY WONDERS

Pyramid Scheme

Summerhill Pyramid Winery is perhaps the most (in)famous winery in Canada. Located in Kelowna, the winery was established in 1991 by Stephen Cipes and is nothing if not grandiose; it features a large pyramid complex that was completed in 1997. The pyramid is made entirely of organic material and is an exact eight-percent-scale replica of the Cheops pyramid in Egypt. The Summerhill pyramid is aligned to true north, not to magnetic north; this was achieved using stars and survey equipment. Rumour also has it that at the exact moment of the pyramid's completion, when the capstone was fused to the frame, two of the workmen's watches stopped simultaneously.

Summerhill features an enormous sparkling-wine bottle pouring a never-ending stream of bubbly into a giant champagne flute. The bottle appears to float in mid-air, without visible support.

Pyramid Power

According to Summerhill owner Stephen Cipes, pyramids have a "profound effect" on liquids placed within them. Cipes conducted taste tests to determine if aging wines in a pyramid had any tangible effect, and the results clearly showed a definite improvement in the pyramid-aged wines. Over three years, Cipes aged some wines in the winery's original 1988 pyramid and some outside of it. He asked visitors to compare the two wines, and the vast majority felt that the pyramid wines were smoother and had better aromas. These results persuaded Cipes to build the Cheops-replica pyramid.

No Quiet Tomb

Although it remains to be seen whether Summerhill's wines really are shaped by cosmic energies, its pyramid has certainly created a buzz: Summerhill is Canada's most-visited winery. Some 1000 tourists stop by the winery every day in the peak season, and more than 55,000 people visit the pyramid each year. Much like the Pyramids of Giza, this wonder of Canada's wine industry is no hidden secret.

On a Mission

Mission Hill Family Estate Winery is one of the Okanagan Valley's mainstays and one of the region's pioneers. It has been voted Canada's Winery of the Year twice, and its large portfolio of wines has garnered dozens of awards worldwide.

It has been featured in wine, travel and architectural media, raising the profile of both Mission Hill and the Okanagan wine industry. No small venture, the estate owns more than 12 percent of BC's vineyard acreage.

The winery recently underwent a six-year-long renovation, costing an estimated $35 million. Proprietor Anthony von Mandl's aim was to create a showcase winery that would remain a landmark for generations. Seattle architect Tom Kundig and a host of other international architects, designers and craftspeople worked together to turn the aged facility into a Tuscan-inspired wonder.

DID YOU  KNOW?

Mission Hill has won the Canadian Winery of the Year award twice, first in 2001 and then in 2007.

Grand Spaces

Arriving at Mission Hill, wine tourists pass through the large entrance gates and under two massive, curved arches hand-chiselled from a five-tonne block of limestone. The arches are held together by a single keystone, which features images from the von Mandl family crest. Perfectly aligned with these arches, such that the top is framed by the graceful curves, is a 12-storey bell tower rising above the courtyard. The tower houses four bronze bells, crafted in France by the Paccard Bell Foundry—whose other work includes bells for New York's St. Patrick's Cathedral and the Sacré Coeur in Paris. Each one of the bells in the Mission Hill tower is dedicated to a member of von Mandl's immediate family. Inside the Chagall Room, a museum-style reception hall, hangs a tapestry by the renowned artist.

Among the winery's numerous other grand components are an open-air terrace with a panoramic view of Lake Okanagan, an estate room housing pieces from the von Mandl family art collection, an outdoor amphitheatre, a 17th-century Renaissance fountain and underground cellars blasted out of volcanic rock.

Old Meets New

Le Clos Jordanne represents the aspirations of many Canadian wineries: to express the Niagara *terroir* in wines that fuse Old World style and tradition with New World innovation. The winery is a joint venture between Vincor Canada and Boisset Vins & Spiriteux, a large French wine and spirits company. The winery partnership was established in 2000, and plans for the new winery were announced in 2002. The ultimate goal of Le Clos Jordanne is to produce Burgundian-style wines in Canada. French viticulturists, all of whom have a strong background in Burgundy, are responsible for managing the vineyards and making the wine. The four vineyards, which are organic, are primarily planted with Pinot Noir, some Chardonnay and a tiny amount of Pinot Gris.

Metal Clouds

Le Clos Jordanne's new winery building, which is slated to open in 2010, is designed by world-renowned architect Frank Gehry. The design features curved, white stucco walls, huge glass columns, suspended catwalks above the vats and a roof of furled metal that Gehry likens to "a silver cloud floating over the vineyard, with the winery spreading out beneath it." The building is multilevel and gravity-flow operated, meaning that the wines will move from section to section without the aid of pumps—a process that yields purer, cleaner wines. The building will be Canada's first complete building designed by Gehry and will no doubt draw lovers of both wine and architecture.

DID YOU  KNOW?

Le Clos Jordanne's new winery was originally scheduled for completion in 2008, but the project was delayed by severe winters that threw off the wine-production schedule. The wine, not the building, takes priority here.

Understated Modernism

Initial impressions of Jackson-Triggs' ultramodern estate winery would have you believe that the operation was some kind of scientific research station. There's no denying that its contemporary design certainly stands out from the quaint, historic buildings dotting the Niagara-on-the-Lake landscape.

Although Jackson-Triggs has been around since 1993, the winery wasn't finished until the summer of 2001. Designed to optimize quality in the winemaking process, the winery was constructed in an efficient, sustainable design. Everything, right down to the floor plan, is state-of-the-art.

Not Your Average Barn

Jackson-Triggs winery's design was inspired by traditional farm buildings, yet it also incorporates decidedly 21st-century influences. The exterior is glass, concrete and stone, allowing plenty of natural light to enter the bright and airy interior. The three-tiered facility is partially gravity-flow assisted and boasts such technologically advanced equipment as rotator fermenters, which periodically roll the fermenting wine to maximize its colour and flavour. The large vaulted underground cellar provides plenty of workspace and also provides elbow room for guests at the winery's frequent dinners and wine tastings.

DID YOU  KNOW?

Despite Niagara's muggy summer heat, the Jackson-Triggs winery does not have central air conditioning. The air is kept cool by circulating it around the cooled stainless steel tanks.

Ontario Gothic

Peninsula Ridge Estate Winery could perhaps be described as an example of "Ontario gothic"—a striking Victorian farmhouse with an almost medieval undercurrent. Purchased in 1999 by Norman Beal, who left a successful career in the petroleum industry to pursue winemaking, Peninsula Ridge almost never came into existence—Beal was close to purchasing a property in California before he consented to his family's urges to settle at home in Canada. He bought the Ontario property for no less than $4.5 million and quickly planted 20 hectares of vineyards. He also built an enormous underground cellar and hired a renowned winemaker, Jean-Pierre Colas.

Cutting-edge Wines

Although Peninsula Ridge's architecture might lull you with its sense of quaint tradition, Jean-Pierre Colas' wines are surprisingly cutting-edge. Colas hails from the Burgundy region of France, where he worked at the famous Chablis winery of Domain Laroche. Instead of working with traditional Burgundian varieties, however, Colas produces one of Niagara's best Sauvignon Blanc wines, as well as a Meritage and several other hearty red wines. Colas also makes Ratafia, a blend of plum juice and grape alcohol modelled on the style of French Mistelle.

WINE APPRECIATION

Winemaking: The Basics

Although making white wine differs slightly from making red wine, both processes start the same way: the grapes are grown, harvested and crushed. The juice released from white-wine grapes flows into a fermenting tank, where yeast bacteria are added. During fermentation, the yeast cells interact with the grape juice's sugars; as the yeast consumes the sugar, it produces alcohol and carbon dioxide as byproducts. Once fermentation is complete, the wine is transferred to another container, where it is aged for a period of time and then bottled.

To make red wine, the juice released during crushing stays in contact with the skins and seeds for a period of time, a process known as maceration. This is where red wine gets its colour—the juice of all grapes is almost colourless. The longer a wine macerates, the darker—and more tannic—it becomes. After maceration, the juice ferments for several days, and the wine is aged and then bottled.

How to Taste Wine

There's no magical secret to tasting wine. It's all about paying attention to your senses—that's it. Grab a glass of wine and go for it.

☞ Sight—Before you do anything, eyeball the wine. Check its colour and compare it to something you're familiar with. For example, a white wine's colour might be described as lemon yellow, straw or amber; a red wine's colour might be cherry red, garnet or rust. Now, look at the rim of the glass, tilting it over something white to more easily see the wine. A greater variation in hue between the wine at the center and the wine at the edge usually means it's older. Wines brown with age, so a brownish rim on a white wine or an orange-brick rim on a red wine indicates a few years of bottle age; a wine that's dark red or pale yellow all the way through is probably younger.

☞ Smell—Give the wine a sniff, without swirling it. Make note of the most obvious aromas. Now give the glass a swirl and take another whiff. Compare the difference in smells: not only does swirling greatly increase the pungency of the aromas, it also releases other aromas that aren't initially detected.

Defining Aromas

When trying to put wine aromas into words, start general and then move into specifics. If a wine smells fruity, try to determine the category of fruit—is it citrus, berry, tropical, tree or dried? Then try to pick out more specific aromas; if a wine smells citrusy, ask yourself if it's more like lemon or lime; if it smells like tree fruit, are you smelling cherries or apples, peaches or apricots?

Here are the basic categories of wine aromas, along with some examples of each:

Fruity
  Citrus: lemon, lime, grapefruit, orange
  Berry: raspberry, strawberry, blackberry
  Tree Fruit: cherry, apple, peach
  Tropical Fruit: pineapple, melon, banana
  Dried Fruit: prune, fig, strawberry jam

Herbaceous/Vegetative
  Fresh: green grass, herbs, bell pepper
  Cooked/Canned: peas, asparagus, olives
  Dried: straw, tea, tobacco
  Floral: violet, rose, geranium

Earthy
  Woody: oak, cedar, vanilla
  Spicy: black pepper, cloves, licorice
  Fungal: mushroom, damp earth
  Nutty: hazelnut, almond, walnut
  Caramel: honey, butterscotch, chocolate, molasses

Chemical
  Lactic: yogurt, sweat, sauerkraut
  Yeasty: dough, baker's yeast
  Sulphur: cabbage, skunk, burnt match, rubber

☛ Taste—Take a sip of the wine, but don't start analyzing it just yet. Rather, use the first sip like mouthwash, to rinse residual tastes in your mouth. You want to have a clean slate against which to judge the wine. Some people prefer to spit out this first mouthful, but there's no reason you can't swallow it. With the second sip, draw in a bit of air with the wine. You'll make a funny gurgling sound, but that's part of the fun—just don't overdo it. Note the wine's predominant flavours, and compare them with the aromas you've already picked out.

☛ Feel—Pay attention to how the wine feels in the mouth. Some of the most important aspects of wine are actually tactile sensations, not flavours. For example, tannins leave your mouth feeling dry and parched, such as when you drink strong tea. A wine that leaves you gasping for water has high tannins. (White wines rarely have tannin, because this component comes from the grape skins.) An acidic wine causes you to salivate after you swallow it, as you do when biting into a lemon. Both white and red wines can be acidic, but it's often more noticeable in whites, because the flavours are often in harmony with the sensation of acid (for example, the wine tastes like citrus fruit). Acidity is an important aspect of red wines, too, however; an acidic red will leave your mouth feeling refreshed and lively.

☛ Spitting—Spitting is acceptable tasting etiquette at most wine-tasting events; buckets or plastic cups are usually provided for this purpose. However, at formal dinners and where no spittoons are provided, you are probably meant to swallow the wine—pace yourself, and be sure to arrange for a ride home before the end of the night.

☛ Faults—When you first look at a wine, check it for obvious faults, such as foreign objects, a strange hue or bubbles in a still wine. This also applies to your first sniff: note any odd smells or distinctly off-putting aromas. A sickly sweet smell, like bad sherry, is an indication of oxidation, which means the wine has been spoiled by too much oxygen. A wine that smells of wet cardboard or damp basement is a sure sign of cork taint, which is caused when a chemical compound that can reside in the cork is released into the wine.

Wine Glasses

Ideally, wine should be served in a clear glass, to allow the drinker to assess its appearance. The glass should also be large enough to allow swirling without spilling. A wide bowl is nice, because it releases more aromas into the glass. The lip of the glass is also important; thinner is better, because it delivers the wine more cleanly onto the palate.

The style of the wine also plays a role in the choice of glass. In general, red wines are served in large, balloon-shaped glasses—the extra air space in these allows the aromas to collect. Serve Champagne in a tall, slender flute, to preserve the bubbles. Dessert wines are traditionally served in short, squat glasses, because the serving size is smaller: only an ounce or two.

The world's most prestigious (and expensive) wine glasses are made by the Austrian company Riedel, which has taken wine appreciation to a completely different level, manufacturing glasses that are tailored to each style of wine. Riedel offers glasses for Bordeaux, Burgundy, Merlot, Shiraz, icewine—you name it and Riedel has designed a specific glass for it! There's no need to keep several boxes of expensive Riedel crystal in the trunk of your car, however, on the odd chance that you're served wine in the "wrong" glass—wine tasting is highly subjective. You can derive equal pleasure from wine served in a plastic tumbler or from elegant crystal.

Decanting

Decanting is the process of pouring wine from the bottle into another vessel. It has two main purposes: first, to remove sediment, and second, to aerate the wine. Some people feel that decanting is absolutely vital; others think it is a waste of time.

Because most wines don't collect sediment until they are a few years old, and young wines usually have none, decanting to remove sediment is not normally an issue for most everyday drinking wines. Aerating the wine is largely subjective; it is thought to increase the wine's aromas and flavours, making it smoother and mellower. However, some feel that this is also largely unimportant for the vast majority of wines. Others say that it makes even the most pedestrian of wines taste better—so, why not decant?

Temperature

Most of us tend to serve our red wines too warm and our white wines too cold. The reason is simple: room temperature is a few degrees too warm for reds, and refrigerator temperature is several degrees too cold for white wines. Red wine should be served at about 15°C. Light-bodied reds are often livelier when chilled at slightly below this temperature. White wine should be served at about 7°C. Sparkling wines can be served a bit colder; dessert wines and full-bodied whites should be served a bit warmer, at about 10°C.

A simple way to get your wines to the right serving temperature is to do a swap about 15 to 20 minutes before you open them— that is, take white out of the fridge about 20 minutes before you open it, and put red in 20 minutes before you want to drink it. In the summer, you might want to double the cooling time for reds, because the wine warms up faster.

Serving Order

When serving wine, the general rule is to serve white wine before red, dry before sweet, light-bodied before full-bodied, young before old and sparkling before still. I'm sure you can already see problems with these rules, because many wines fall into more than one category. Use your own judgment—if you happen to sip something that clashes horribly with what came before, have a few mouthfuls of water and a bite of food—preferably something bland, such as bread or crackers—to cleanse your palate.

Wine Pairing

Entire books have been written about the subject of wine and food pairing. There are many things to know, and years of trial and error are required to really become a master at it. However, by following a few basic rules, you can avoid creating truly hideous combinations. Remember to take the process with a grain of salt—even if the pairing flops, the meal won't be ruined.

The following tips for pairing food and wine can help you avoid the most common blunders:

☞ Play matchmaker—try to match the predominant flavours and textures of the wine with those in the dish. For example, pair citrusy Sauvignon Blanc with fish cooked with lemon; creamy Chardonnay with chicken in cream sauce; plummy Merlot with velvety lamb; and tannic Cabernet Sauvignon with hearty red meat.

☞ Choose a wine with high acidity—to make a good partner to food, wines need a high degree of acidity to cleanse the palate between bites. Insufficient acidity muddies the flavours of the wine and the food—it's the equivalent of sticking a multicourse meal in a blender and hitting frappe.

☛ Pay attention to tannins—an extremely tannic red wine will not taste good with most foods, for example. However, some degree of tannin is necessary when pairing a wine with heavy dishes, especially red meats. Cabernet Sauvignon, Syrah and Sangiovese are examples of fairly tannic reds that work well with heavy meat dishes. Salt decreases the perception of tannins. If a wine is too tannic, pair it with something salty; the salt will make the wine taste more mellow and less aggressive. Decanting the wine also helps smooth out its tannins.

☛ Spicy foods are best matched with sweeter wines; the sweetness helps quell some of the heat. However, for truly intense spice, you are better off with a glass of milk—no wine is a good match for those five-alarm chicken wings.

☛ The wine should be sweeter than the food. This is especially important when picking a wine to go with dessert. If the dish is sweeter than the wine, the wine will taste thin and acidic.

☛ When in doubt, go with bubbles. Sparkling wines pair well with many foods, especially fried or greasy dishes.

☛ Have fun! Wine and food pairing isn't an exact science, and even if something really doesn't jive, you'll have learned something valuable.

HOW TO SPEAK WINE

A Wine Glossary

A lot of terms can get tossed around in a wine conversation, many that can be confusing to the aspiring wine drinker. Wine has its own unique vocabulary, and it helps to know some of the basics. Below are some of the most common wine terms.

Acidity: the level of tartness in a wine. Wines contain several types of acid, namely acetic, citric, lactic, malic and tartaric, which contribute to the wine's structure. Wines high in acidity are more refreshing than those with low acidity. Acidity is perceived as a tart sensation, similar to the experience of biting into a lemon.

Aeration: allowing a wine to come into contact with air. Letting a wine "breathe" releases more of its aromas and flavours.

Appellation: the official name for a wine's area of origin. Each country has its own appellation laws but most are based on France's Appellation d'Origine Contrôlée (AOC). Canada's appellation system is the Vintners Quality Alliance (VQA).

Body: the weight of the wine in the mouth, ranging from light-bodied to medium-bodied and full-bodied.

Botrytis/noble rot: a fungal disease that attacks the skins of grapes and causes the water to evaporate, concentrating the sugars and acids in the berries. Wines made from such grapes are sweet and rich dessert-style wines.

Dry: the opposite of sweet; a wine in which the sugars have been fully fermented.

Finish: the final impression—in both taste and sensation—left by the wine after swallowing (or spitting).

Fortification: adding brandy or other neutral spirits to a wine to stop fermentation, resulting in a sweet wine. Port is an example of a fortified wine.

Legs: the drops of wine that cling to and eventually run down the sides of the glass after swirling. Their thickness and speed can indicate the wine's alcohol and sugar content; slow-moving legs usually mean the wine is lower in alcohol and higher in residual sugar, and vice-versa.

Must: the mixture of unfermented grape juice and solids created at the initial crushing of grapes.

Nose: the smell of a wine, also called its bouquet or aroma.

Oaky: the taste and smell of oak in a wine, which can range from vanilla and coconut (common with American oak) to toast and baking spices (common with French oak).

Palate: the effect of wine on the whole mouth that can also be described as the taste of wine.

Phylloxera: a sap-sucking insect that feeds on the roots of grapevines and eventually causes it to die. During the late 1800s, this pest destroyed between two-thirds and nine-tenths of Europe's vineyards. Almost all the world's vines are now grafted onto the rootstocks of resistant grape species.

Tannin: a bitter compound that naturally occurs in the skins, seeds and stalks of grapes, which is imparted to wine during pressing and maceration (skin contact). White wines have little or no tannins, because the juice usually does not remain in contact with the skins or seeds. Tannins are perceived on the palate as an astringent, drying sensation.

Terroir: a French term denoting the conditions in the vine's growing environment, including soil, location and climate.

Weight: how heavy the wine feels in the mouth. Heavier wines are typically higher in alcohol.

Vintage: the year in which the grapes were harvested.

DID YOU  KNOW?

The German word to describe the legs of a wine is *kirchenfenster* (church windows); the Spanish use the word *lagrimas* (tears).

LABEL LANGUAGE

Decoding the Label

Luckily for us, Canadian wine labels are not nearly as compli-
cated as those from, say, France. Information is (usually) clearly
laid out and readily accessible. However, wine is a fairly esoteric
product, at least, at first glance, so a certain degree of knowledge can definitely help navigate the average wine label. Here
are some tips for decoding Canadian wine labels.

☛ Name of winery—The winery's name usually appears in
large font in the top section of the label on the front of the
bottle. Occasionally, the brand name, not the winery name,
is featured in large print; in this case, the winery's name is
usually found at the bottom of the front label.

☛ Name of wine—This is where the producer and marketer
get creative; you'll find all manner of weird and wonderful
names adorning the labels of Canadian wine. Note that
the grape variety is often used in place of a name.

☛ Vintage date—The vintage is the year the grapes were harvested, not the year the wine was bottled, which can occur
some time later. If the wine is a blend of two or more vintages,
the date will not appear on the label, and the designation
NV (non-vintage) might stand in its place.

☛ VQA abbreviation—A wine certified by the Vintners Quality
Alliance (VQA) bears the VQA abbreviation on the bottle.
A VQA certification guarantees that 100 percent of the grapes
used to make the wine were grown in the stated region.

☛ Region—The region is the area in which the grapes were
grown. If stated, it must be one of Canada's seven Designated
Viticultural Areas (DVA). These DVAs are Niagara Peninsula,

Pelee Island, Lake Erie North Shore, Prince Edward County, Okanagan Valley, Similkameen Valley and Fraser Valley.

☞ Contents—The contents describes the type of wine in the bottle: for example, red wine, white wine, dessert wine. The description must be written in both English and French.

☞ Alcoholic content—This number indicates how much heat the wine is packing. It is the amount of alcohol in the wine by volume.

☞ National origin—All Canadian wines are labelled Product of Canada, in both English and French.

☞ Liquid measure—This is simply the amount of wine in the bottle, in metric. A standard bottle contains 750 mL; half-bottles hold 375 mL.

☞ Back label—The back label is where winemakers and producers can wax poetic and provide additional information—some of which can actually be pertinent—about their product.

DID YOU  KNOW?

Someone who collects wine labels is called a vintitulist.

Product of…Chile?
Although absences are usually harder to notice than mistakes, the missing information on a wine label speaks volumes—often telling you more about the wine than the information that's actually present. This is especially true with cheaper wines.

One of the most important pieces of information about a wine is where it is grown and made. If a wine label does not state regional information, other than Product of Canada, the wine might contain only 30 percent Canadian grapes—which means that 70 percent of the grapes used to make the wine

were grown elsewhere—often in California, though it is not uncommon for Canadian producers to source grapes from such far away countries as Chile. Legislation allowing this hefty amount of foreign juice was passed in 1988, as a result of the Free Trade Agreement with the United States; it was part of a government policy to help vintners adjust to the newly competitive open market.

DID YOU  KNOW?

In 2005, there was such a shortage of grapes in Ontario that the portion of Ontario grapes required to be added to imported bulk wine was reduced to only one percent.

Non-vintage Wines

Most Canadian wines state the vintage on the label. Some, however, do not. A label with no stated vintage indicates a wine that was made from a blend of vintages. This is not necessarily a bad thing; indeed, it is often a very good thing, especially in cold growing regions. Most wines produced in Québec and Nova Scotia, for example, do not state a vintage because they are almost always blends of wines from different years.

Blending vintages allows the producer to achieve consistency in style. Because Canada's climate is so harsh, and grapes fail to ripen fully in many years, blending wines allows producers to make a consistent product, regardless of what Mother Nature throws at them. Although grape quality is less of a problem in the warmer regions of British Columbia and Ontario, wines from these areas are also made in this way. Wineries commonly make entry-level wines from blended vintages; the method allows the winery to achieve a consistent style year after year.

DID YOU  KNOW?

The vast majority of French Champagne is non-vintage. In fact, Champagne producers are required by law to withhold a percentage of their wine each year, so that it can be blended with other vintages.

Vintners Quality Alliance (VQA)

The Vintners Quality Alliance is a provincially run organization, which means that the rules are slightly different in Ontario than they are in British Columbia. However, they are almost identical, because BC modelled its system on Ontario's. Ontario implemented its VQA in 1988, BC in 1990. The VQA's main purpose is to set standards for wine through a series of regulations that wines must meet to gain the VQA designation. The hope is that, one day, the VQA will become a federal system, because the current provincially based system has been a major impediment to getting Canadian wines into the lucrative European market.

DID YOU  KNOW?

British Columbia VQA wine sales have doubled in the last six years to more than $155 million annually.

VQA Regulations

Wines must meet many different regulations to become VQA certified. Here is a list of the most important requirements common to both Ontario and British Columbia's VQA:

☛ Permissible grape varieties are limited to *Vitis vinifera* and a few premium hybrids.

☛ Grapes must attain minimum levels of ripeness before harvest.

☛ To be labelled as a varietal wine (a wine named after the grape variety), the wine must contain at least 85 percent of that variety.

☛ To carry a VQA designation, 85 percent of the wine must come from that region.

☛ To carry a specific vineyard designation, 100 percent of the wine must come from that vineyard.

☛ Wineries must submit their wines to an independent tasting panel for evaluation before obtaining VQA designation.

WINE MISCELLANEA

Ouch!

In 1974, Canadian actor Christopher Plummer said the following about Canadian wines: "My God, they're terrible! I had a glass on the train from Montréal, and my hand nearly fell off." At a Canada Day celebration in 1975, an unnamed British diplomat took a sip of the Canadian "Champagne" being served and declared that it was "fit only for launching enemy submarines."

DID YOU KNOW?

Canada ranks just ahead of the United States in per capita consumption of wine: each Canadian drinks roughly 10 bottles of wine per year. The country at the top of the list is Luxembourg, whose citizens each drink more than 84 bottles of wine a year—just ahead of France at 80 bottles per person.

Cheesy Comments

Not everyone agrees on the factors contributing to the increase in wine consumption in Canada over the last 40 years. Take Percy Rowe, who, in his 1970 book *Wines of Canada*, claims that wine and cheese parties "have brought the most notable single change in Canadian drinking patterns in recent times. There are so many of these parties because they are initially easy for the host and hostess to arrange, and because Canada is one of the few countries to produce both good cheese and good wine. All that is necessary is a few bottles of wine, usually dry and sweet, red and white, and a rosé or two for the women guests." Clearly Rowe would be booed off the stage for making such chauvinistic comments in contemporary times, but you can't deny his enthusiasm for Canada's local juice.

Wine Non-appreciation

In 1977, wine critic and author Andrew Sharp made a bold suggestion and condemned "anti-wine snobs" for their flagrant disregard for wine. Sharp described these anti-wine snobs rather hilariously as a group comprised mainly of Canadian males who view an appreciation of wine as akin to "riding side-saddle" and who can be identified as "the one who approaches the listing board or stocked shelves with the same pained expression so evident on the faces of husbands whose trip to the drug store included buying sanitary napkins for the wife."

French Acceptance

On July 8, 1867, a week after Canada became an independent nation, the *Toronto Leader* printed a glowing story about the reception of Canadian wines at a French wine exposition. This admiration was notable because, at the time, Canada's wine industry was still in its infancy, and its wines would not be recognized in France or anywhere else outside of Canada's borders for more than a century.

*The French exposition has established the character of
our Canadian wines. The jury on wines, which would
naturally be composed of the best judges to be found in
Europe, speak in very high terms of the wines sent from
the Clair House Vineyards, Cooksville. They find in
them a resemblance to the Beaujolais wine, which is
known to be the best produced in France. They say of
those wines that 'they are pure and of excellent quality,
and solve the problem of Canada being able to furnish
good wines.' This authoritative opinion of the quality of
Ontario wine will do more than anything else that could
possibly occur, at present, to bring this wine into general
use... The time will come, we hope and verily believe,
when grape-growing and wine-making will be one of
the principal employments of our population.*

Great Lakes Pit Stop

Barnes Wines Ltd. was one of Canada's oldest and longest-operating wineries; it opened in 1873 in Niagara and didn't close until 1988. The company's records include evidence of some of Canada's earliest winery tourists in the form of Great Lakes skippers, who left their ships to be towed through the canal by mules, while they visited Barnes to sample the wines. No doubt this was so they could choose the best wine for their captain's table.

Jailhouse Wine

In 2005, the Central East Correctional Centre in Lindsay, Ontario, refused to let a Catholic priest bring in wine to celebrate mass with Catholic prisoners. Father Jim Serceley alleged that discrimination was preventing him from carrying out this fundamental aspect of the Catholic faith, and the subsequent storm of controversy was swift and vehement. This wasn't the first time Central East had prohibited sacramental wine—in a previous incident that received much less media attention, members of the Anglican clergy were prevented from celebrating Eucharist with prisoners, because the ceremony used wine. However, the presence of sacramental wine was not a problem in other jails throughout Ontario, so the issue was quickly brought to a close. Within a few weeks, a new policy was instated, allowing priests to bring in a small amount of wine for sacramental use.

Killer Temperatures

Although it boasts high summer temperatures, the Okanagan region can experience bitterly cold winters, and because most grape varieties cannot survive temperatures lower than –20°C, this often spells disaster. The winter of 1955–56 was notoriously chilly: temperatures as low as –22°C were recorded throughout the Okanagan, resulting in a decrease in production the following year by 78 percent. In December 1964, lows of –26°C were recorded (rather ironically) in Summerland. This time, the damage was nearly total; production was down 94 percent the next year. The winter of 1978–79 was also very cold; more than half of British Columbia's vines were killed.

DID YOU KNOW?

Canada's taxes on wine are the highest in the world—they are more than twice as high as the taxes in the runner-up, New Zealand.

Going Organic

British Columbia offers organic certification for wineries and grape growers under several different certification bodies, which operate collectively under Certified Organic Associations of BC (COABC). As of 2009, 19 vineyards and wineries in British Columbia had obtained full organic certification:

Baccata Ridge Winery

Baessler Farm

Barking Dog Organic Vineyard

Beaumont Estate Vineyards

Cottrill Vineyard

Forbidden Fruit Winery

Heart Achers

Hollywood & Wine

Hyndman Vineyard

Mulberry Farm

Park Hill Vineyards

Rolling Sage Orchard

Rollingdale Vineyard & Winery

Rothe Orchards

SoleTerre Vineyards

Summer Gate Winery

Summerhill Estate Winery

Sundance Organic Farms

Working Horse Winery & Vineyard

Only one Ontario winery is certified organic: Frogpond Farm, which is certified through Organic Crop Producers & Processors. Similarly, only one winery in Nova Scotia, L'Acadie Vineyards, is certified organic.

NOTES ON SOURCES

Aspler, Tony. *The Wine Atlas of Canada*. Toronto: Random House Canada, 2006.

—. *Travels with my Corkscrew*: Memoirs of a Wine Lover. Whitby: McGraw-Hill Ryerson, 1997.

—. *Vintage Canada: The Complete Reference to Canadian Wines*, 3rd ed. Toronto: McGraw-Hill Ryerson, 1999.

Aspler, Tony, and Barbara Leslie. *Canadian Wine for Dummies*. Toronto: CDG Books Canada, 2000.

Brooks, Andrew. *Crush on Niagara: The Definitive Wine Tour Guide*. North Vancouver: Whitecap Books, 2005.

de Courtenay, J.M. *The Canada Vine Grower: How Every Farmer in Canada May Plant a Vineyard and Make His Own Wine*. Toronto: James Campbell & Son, 1866. (microfiche)

Hainle, Sandra. "Ruthless Predators," *BC Wine Country: The Book*. Cindy Wagner and Karin Hanna, eds. Kelowna: Blue Moose, 2000.

Kaufman, William I. *Encyclopedia of American Wine including Mexico and Canada*. Los Angeles: Jeremy P. Tarcher, 1984.

Phillips, Rod. *Ontario Wine Country*. North Vancouver: Whitecap Books, 2006.

Rannie, William F. *Wines of Ontario: An Industry Comes of Age*. Lincoln: W.F. Rannie, 1978.

Rowe, Percy. *The Wines of Canada*. Toronto: McGraw Hill Company of Canada Limited, 1970.

Schreiner, John. "History of the British Columbia Wine Industry," *BC Wine Country: The Book.* Cindy Wagner and Karin Hanna, eds. Kelowna: Blue Moose, 2000.

—. *The British Columbia Wine Companion.* Victoria: Orca Book Publishers, 1996.

—. *The Wineries of British Columbia.* North Vancouver: Whitecap Books, 2004.

—. *The Wines of Canada.* London: Octopus Publishing Group, 2005.

Sendzik, Walter, and Christopher Waters. *Vines: Buyer's Guide to Canadian Wine.* 3rd ed. St. Catharines: Vines Publishing, 2003.

Sharp, Andrew. *Vineland 1000.* Toronto: Andrew Sharp Publications, 1977.

Steinke, Gord. *Mobsters & Rumrunners of Canada: Crossing the Line.* Edmonton: Folklore Publishing, 2003.

Ziraldo, Donald. *Icewine: Extreme Winemaking.* Toronto: Key Porter Books, 2007.

WEBSITES

archives.cbc.ca/economy_business/consumer_goods/topics/1041-5824/

www.andreswines.com

www.bcwine.ca

www.blastedchurch.com

www.bluegrousevineyards.com

www.canadianoak.com

www.canwine.com/index.html

www.celebritycellars.com

www.certifiedorganic.bc.ca

www.chateaudescharmes.com

www.chwta.org

www.danaykroydwines.com

www.domainedechaberton.com

www.domainedelileronde.com

www.domainepinnacle.com

www.elephantislandwine.com

www.ensantewinery.com

www.erobertparker.com

www.featherstonewinery.ca

www.grandprewines.ns.ca

www.grapegrowersofontario.com

www.graymonk.com

www.gretzky.com/wine

www.henryofpelham.com

www.inniskillin.com

www.intermiel.com

www.jacksontriggswinery.com

www.jostwine.com

www.labauge.com

www.laughingstock.ca

www.leclosjordanne.com

www.littlefatwino.com/awc.html

www.longdog.ca

www.mackenzieinstitute.com/1997/1997_10_Sex_Alcohol.html

www.megalomaniacwine.com

www.mikeweirwine.com

www.missionhillwinery.com

www.nataliemaclean.com

www.nkmipcellars.com

www.peleeisland.com

www.redroosterwinery.com

www.rochedesbrises.com

www.rollingstonesicewine.com

www.peninsularidge.com

www.quailsgate.com

www.rodrigueswinery.com

www.summerhill.bc.ca

www.tdg.ca/ontag/grape

www.vqaontario.com

www.wildasswines.com

www.winebc.com

www.wineroute.com

www.winespectator.com

www.winesofcanada.com

www.winesofquebec.com

www.wonderwine.net

ABOUT THE AUTHOR

Melissa Priestley

Although not raised in a wine-drinking family—the first wine she ever tried was a lowly Canadian jug wine served at the Thanksgiving table when she was 14—Melissa Priestley has more than made up for her lack of early experience with the grape. She started working in the liquor industry at the ripe old age of 18, as an employee at a couple of wine boutiques. She has since gone on to write a weekly wine column for *See* magazine and become a certified sommelier through the Court of Master Sommeliers. Melissa lives in Edmonton, Alberta, with her husband, Matt, and their cat, Jazz.

ABOUT THE ILLUSTRATOR

Roger Garcia

Roger Garcia is a self-taught artist with some formal training who specializes in cartooning and illustration. He is an immigrant from El Salvador, and during the last few years, his work has been primarily cartoons and editorial illustrations in pen and ink. Recently, he has started painting once more. Focusing on simplifying the human form, he uses a bright, minimal palette and as few elements as possible. His work can be seen in newspapers, magazines, promo material and on www.rogergarcia.ca.

BLUE BIKE BOOKS MORE TRIVIA FROM BLUE BIKE BOOKS...

FOR THE LOVE OF COFFEE
by Karen Rowe

Coffee has evolved from a dark brew made from a little brown bean into a veritable art form of lattes, mochas, espressos, cappuccinos, moccaccinos and a host of other coffee-based concoctions. This book shares the rich and sometimes violent history of coffee, along with an overflowing cup of interesting coffee trivia. A great gift book!

$14.95 • ISBN: 978-1-897278-65-9 • 5.25" x 8.25" • 224 pages

CANADIAN BOOK OF BEER
by Steve Cameron

Crack open the stories behind our unofficial national beverage. From brewing company feuds to the history of hops to where to buy your suds and recycle the empties, our country has more energy dedicated to the brewing tradition than you might realize. So, drink up!

$14.95 • ISBN: 978-1-897278-64-2 • 5.25" x 8.25" • 224 pages

FOR THE LOVE OF CHOCOLATE
by Karen Rowe

Chocolate. Seductive, decadent and sinfully delicious. The pages of this book are dripping with an assortment of facts, trivia and history about the world's favourite indulgence. If you are a serious chocoholic or even just the occasional nibbler, satisfy your sweet tooth and feed your appetite for learning about the "food of the gods."

$14.95 • ISBN: 978-1-897278-56-7 • 5.25" x 8.25" • 224 pages

BRIDE'S BOOK OF TRADITIONS, TRIVIA & CURIOSITIES
by Rachel Conard and Lisa Wojna

People all over the world have developed much tradition and folklore surrounding weddings, including rituals and superstitions. This book is a highly entertaining look at the many curious practices that have grown up around the marriage rite.

$14.95 • ISBN: 978-1-897278-51-2 • 5.25" x 8.25" • 224 pages

Available from your local bookseller or
by contacting the distributor,

Lone Pine Publishing
1-800-661-9017

www.lonepinepublishing.com